A Concise Guide to
BUTTERFLIES
& MOTHS

A CONCISE GUIDE TO

BUTTERFLIES & MOTHS

Elizabeth Balmer

Bath · New York · Singapore · Hong Kong · Cologne · Delhi · Melbourne

This is a Parragon Book
First published in 2007

Parragon Books Ltd
Queen Street House
4 Queen Street
Bath, BA1 1HE

Produced by Atlantic Publishing

See page 256 for
photograph copyright details
Text © Parragon Books Ltd 2006

ISBN 978-1-4054-8798-6
Printed in China

CONTENTS

INTRODUCTION 10

PAPILIONIDAE – SWALLOWTAILS 30–43

PIERIDAE – WHITES AND SULPHURS 44–67

LYCENIDAE – GOSSAMER WINGS 68–93

NYMPHALIDAE BRUSHFOOTS 94–156

HESPERIIDAE – SKIPPERS 158–169

SATYRIIDAE – SATYRS AND BROWNS 170–187

MOTHS 188–237

INTRODUCTION

Butterflies and moths tend to elicit a range of emotions in us, from wonder at their incredible beauty, their ability to metamorphose or their unbelievable feats of physical achievement, to dismay at their voracious appetites for our crops and clothing. For many of us, simply observing butterflies skipping across the flowers in our gardens is pleasure enough; however, the world of butterflies and moths is full of remarkable and often unknown facts and details.

Butterflies and moths belong to the order Lepidoptera. This Greek word translates as 'scales' and 'wing': the most obvious feature that separates them from other orders of insects is their scaled wings. There are in excess of 160,000 known species of Lepidoptera in the world, and only about 10 per cent of these are butterflies. They can survive in an incredibly diverse range of habitats, from frozen Arctic tundra to high-altitude mountain slopes to humid rainforests. It is perhaps this diversity and adaptability that has enabled the Lepidoptera to survive on the planet for the last 140 million years. The first Lepidoptera were primitive moths; butterflies evolved around 40 million years ago.

The object of this book is to provide a glimpse into the fascinating world of butterflies and moths, using a very small selection of the known species that currently inhabit our planet. Each butterfly entry points out the significant features of an individual species which can either aid identification or simply illustrate some of its more interesting attributes.

Right: A Malachite butterfly (Metamorpha stelenes) *on a leaf with its wings closed. Its common name comes from the beautiful green of its wings with their strong veining, which is reminiscent of the semi-precious stone malachite.*

Above: Lepidoptra have two pairs of wings with a wide range of different colours and patterns that are an important factor when identifying the species.

Identification

Butterflies and moths are members of the insect class, sharing the same key features of three pairs of legs and three body parts: head, thorax and abdomen. In addition to these features, Lepidoptera also have two pairs of wings, the forewings and hindwings, which are covered with scales. These scales reflect light, revealing the colours and patterns that are so important when identifying different species. The pair of antennae on the head of the butterfly is the primary sense organ, receiving smells, pheromones and vibrations. A butterfly's proboscis is its tongue, enabling it to suck up food, nutrients and moisture. It is hollow and contains two parallel tubes; the end bears the taste sensors. Different species will have different lengths of proboscis: some members of the hawk moth family have a proboscis that exceeds their own body length and is capable of piercing fruit or beehives, whereas others, such as the luna moths, have no mouthparts at all and cannot feed as adults. Another organ is the labial palps, used to clean the proboscis and eyes and to sense and taste food; the American Snout butterfly has particularly large palps. The head also bears a pair of compound eyes, capable of detecting colour and movement. The jointed legs contain sensors at the 'feet' which enable a butterfly to identify the plant it has just landed on, particularly important for females that need to lay eggs on a specific host plant.

Probably the first point of observation when identifying a butterfly or moth is the colour and patterning that is displayed on the wings. When a butterfly is in flight this can be particularly difficult to do; it is when at rest that we get the opportunity to closely examine the markings of a particular species. Look for the colouring, any significant patterns, eyespots or markings. The majority of butterflies hold their wings closed above their bodies, leaving only the underside visible; some will hold their wings out flat, perhaps sunning themselves, affording us a glimpse of their often more brightly coloured upper side. The colour of the body can also be a useful feature: many species show abdomens that are highly coloured or banded, or have markings on the head or thorax. The keen lepidopterist should also notice the size and shape of the butterfly, whether there are any wing streamers, or tails, and the general shape of the wings: broad, narrow, pointed, rounded, scalloped or fringed.

Below: The size and shape of a butterfly's body and wings are also a clue to identification. This Nymph Sailor (Neptis hylas) has pointed forewings and rounded hindwings.

Be aware when attempting identification that individual species can vary in appearance. Newly emerged or fresh butterflies can have brighter colours, whereas older specimens can have faded wings, or even show wear and tear. Butterflies appearing in different seasons can vary, and many species can vary depending on whether they are from a first brood or a later one. Males and females of the same species can also differ, either completely or only slightly, perhaps in size or colour tone. Then of course there are butterflies that vary between different regions, confusingly appearing in a number of different forms. Where appropriate, any variations in appearance have been included in the descriptions provided here.

Butterfly or moth?

In some respects the differences between butterflies and moths may seem rather arbitrary. Although moths are regarded as the butterflies' less colourful, less attractive cousins, there are a great many beautiful, highly coloured daytime-flying moths. Conversely, a large number of butterflies can appear rather dull and insignificant, and are often mistaken for moths. There are, however, a number of general features that separate moths from butterflies.

Butterflies are diurnal – daytime – fliers, whereas the great majority of moths are nocturnal, flying and (if appropriate) feeding at night. They also differ structurally: when resting, the wings of butterflies are usually held together upwards over the back of the body, whereas moths will fold their wings flat across the body, the hindwing tucked beneath the forewing. In flight, the wings of the moth are 'coupled' together with the use of special bristles on the hindwing which catch hold of the forewing. Butterflies lack this feature; instead their hindwing is expanded underneath the forewing, providing support with which to fly. The

*Above: Butterflies, such as this Monarch (*Danaus plexippus*), typically rest with their wings upright and have slender antennae that are clubbed at the end. They also tend to have more slender bodies than moths, which are often stocky in shape.*
*Opposite: Eastern Tiger Swallowtails (*Papilo glaucus*) in two different colours.*

antennae of each also differ: butterflies have very slender antennae which are clubbed at the end; moths lack this clubbing, having either slim or feathered antennae. Butterflies also tend to have more slender bodies, whereas some moths can be very stocky and broad in shape. There are, of course, exceptions to all these rules: the colourful daytime moths of the Uranidae family and the Australian Regent Skipper butterfly with its moth-like wing-coupling device are just two examples among many.

Conservation

With so many different species of butterfly and moth in existence, it can be hard to believe that they are seriously threatened. However, a number of fascinating and beautiful butterflies and moths are in peril, from either habitat change or over-zealous collectors. As people become increasingly interested in observing and recording sightings of butterflies, efforts to conserve species have increased.

Loss of native habitats is the most serious threat. On a large scale, massive deforestation, such as in Central America and Asia, can affect many different species. However, even on a small scale, many butterflies rely on plants that we consider weeds, such as nettles, thistles or dandelions. The use of pesticides can have a harmful effect on some species, and pesticides that target destructive butterflies, such as the Gypsy moth, are also responsible for the near-eradication of other, innocent, species. There are some conservation measures in place: many species are legally protected from collectors; others have been reintroduced into native environments. However, many butterflies and moths remain under threat of extinction.

Using this guide

The entries provide a tiny example of the more common or unusual butterfly and moth species. Each entry contains a general description of the butterfly: where it is a uniform pattern or colour just the upper side is described, but if there is a difference between upper and lower sides this is clearly explained. Differences between the sexes are also described, although only one example may be seen in the picture. Other information included can be useful for identification purposes: the average wingspan of the adult, its typical habitat and range, and the likelihood of observing it – its 'status'. Brief details on the caterpillar and its host plant are provided, since this can enhance identification; many butterflies choose to live in habitats where their larval host plant is found. The entries are organized into butterflies and moths, then into each major family. The huge numbers of moths mean only a small sample of the many families is represented here. Large families of butterflies are organized into sub-families. All the entries use the species' common name, which can vary from region to region; scientific names are consistent across the world.

*Opposite: A Queen Butterfly (*Danaus gilippus*) resting on a flower.*

THE LIFE OF
THE BUTTERFLY

LIFE-CYCLE

There are four stages in the life cycle of all Lepidoptera – egg, caterpillar, pupa and butterfly – and each stage is vital. Butterflies are not simply attractive pollinators of garden flowers: their ultimate goal is to mate and successfully reproduce; likewise, caterpillars must not only feed and store up energy, they also have to ensure they are not the victims of hungry predators.

Laid singly, in small groups or in huge numbers, eggs can take either a few days or several weeks to hatch. They can be one of a number of shapes, colours and even sizes: some eggs are tiny, others surprisingly large. Eggs are usually laid on specific host plants by the female butterfly, which walks across the plant surface using the sensors in her legs to determine it is the correct one. Less fussy eggs can be released in flight, particularly those whose caterpillars feed upon grass. Once the egg hatches, the newly emerged caterpillar begins by eating the hard shell, then it gets to work eating its host plant.

*Above: The eggs of a Large White (*Pieris brassicae*) on a leaf.*
Opposite: The pupa is vulnerable to predators, so it is often very well camouflaged to look like the fruit or bud on a plant.

Caterpillars also appear in a wide variety of sizes, shapes and colours. They are particularly vulnerable to predators: birds, other insects and lizards are among the many animals that prey on these butterfly larvae, and so their appearance is often determined by their need to protect themselves. Poisonous caterpillars may appear brightly coloured to ward off attack, or bear aggressive spines that can irritate if touched or ingested. The caterpillars of the Arctid moth family are particularly hairy and collectively referred to as 'woolly bears'. Some caterpillars display very unusual and somewhat aggressive features, such as horns, alarming tail whips and false eyespots. Many Swallowtail caterpillars have an organ called an osmaterium, rather like an inflatable horn, which releases a repulsive scent. The caterpillar of the Puss moth has a number of these aggressive attributes, and can also spit formic acid for good measure. Many other caterpillars adopt rather more passive but equally successful methods of protecting themselves from predators, either adopting camouflage or simply hiding within or beneath the foliage.

Caterpillars spend most of their time eating, and as their bodies grow they slough off their skin, rather like a snake. Most caterpillars will shed their skin several times before they are large enough to begin pupating. For most species, this means that the final skin-shedding reveals not another caterpillar but its chrysalis or cocoon. For others, particularly moths, the chrysalis is spun from a single strand of silk, encasing the caterpillar in a protective shell so that it can begin its transformation.

Once the caterpillar has revealed or spun its chrysalis, it enters the pupa stage. As a pupa, it is extremely vulnerable to predators since it is completely immobile; consequently pupae will adopt a number of strategies to protect themselves. Most pupae are incredibly well camouflaged, resembling dry leaves, twigs, fresh buds and even bird droppings, such as those of the Swallowtail family. Some pupa casings are covered with spines while others containing a poisonous butterfly will advertise their inedible status. Many species pupate underground, within plant roots or even inside ants' nests, such as the Large Blue butterfly pupa. It usually takes around two weeks for

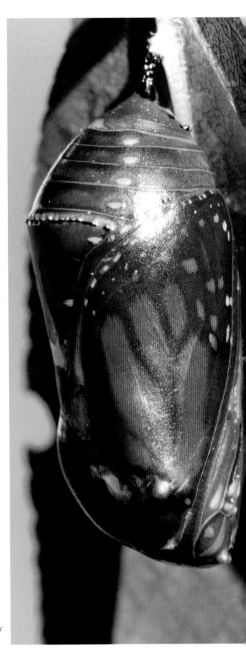

Opposite: Caterpillar of a Monarch butterfly (Danaus plexippus) *on milkweed.*
Right: The wing colours of a Monarch can clearly be seen through this transparent chrysalis.

pupation to complete, although some species can take much longer — several months or even two years, depending on external circumstances.

Once metamorphosis is complete, the butterfly must break out of the chrysalis. At this stage the wings are crumpled up; it is the body that must be forced out of the shell. As the butterfly takes in air for the first time, its thorax and abdomen can expand and its wings can begin to swell. The wings are composed of two membranes which are fed by veins, and as these fill up so the wings are expanded to take on their final shape. However, before it flies, the fresh butterfly must allow its wings to dry out and harden, a process that can take several hours.

Behaviour

The lifespan of a butterfly varies from species to species. Some live for less than a week, others long enough to migrate through the winter months. But the typical adult butterfly will, during its lifetime, fly, feed, mate and migrate.

Feeding butterflies use their proboscis to suck up liquid nutrients such as flower nectar, tree sap, rotten fruit juices, honeydew, blood and faecal liquid and even, in some cases, animal tears. Some male butterflies, such as the Blue Triangle, will feed from the mud found in puddles or on riverbanks, probably seeking extra nutrients necessary for reproduction.

*Above and opposite: A Monarch butterfly (*Danaus plexippus*) emerging from its chrysalis. Its wings have been crumpled inside so the butterfly must rest to allow them to expand and harden.*

Reproduction can only take place when butterflies of the same species successfully identify one another. This can be particularly tricky when different species look similar or when the environment makes it awkward to spot a potential mate. Some butterflies are dependent upon their pheromones or scent to entice their partner, others will engage in elaborate courtship displays which communicate compatibility as well as general suitability. Mating pairs will clasp together, either landed or in air, and can remain attached for anything from twenty minutes to twenty-four hours. The male then usually heads off in search of a new mate while the female begins to search for a suitable place to deposit her eggs.

The majority of butterflies remain within the same territory for their whole lives, being able to satisfy their needs within their chosen habitat and range. However, some species migrate across relatively long distances in order to take advantage of potential food sources in other areas. During warm periods butterflies will migrate in order to follow the fine weather; for instance, the Monarch, a well-

known migrant, will head north across the North American continent, following the spread of new flowers brought by spring. In most cases, the butterflies that migrate out of their range do not return home; instead the next generation heads back to the native area as the seasons change. In Europe, well known migrant butterflies include Pale Clouded Yellows and Painted Ladies; these are generally native to North Africa and Mediterranean Europe but can regularly be found as far north as Scandinavia during the summer months. Other butterflies, such as the Red Admiral, migrate in order to overwinter, or to hibernate. They seek out temperate but cool climates where they can remain, safely immobile, reserving their energy until the arrival of spring. The onset of winter is a challenge that all species of butterfly and moth have to face. Different species cope with this period when little or no food is available in particular ways. Many overwinter as eggs, or choose this time to pupate; those that are already adults may hibernate; some caterpillars, too, are able to shut down their metabolism to wait out the winter months.

Habitat

The relationship between butterflies and their habitat is crucial; particular habitats are chosen by individual species because they have evolved adaptations suitable to those habitats.

All Lepidoptera need warmth to provide them with the energy to fly; therefore butterflies are found in sunny, tropical and temperate regions. They will need specific foods both for breeding and for the adults to feed. Typical habitats will therefore be places such as open woodland, where the sunlight can penetrate and where there are plentiful flowers, or meadows and grassland, heathland and coasts with their specific flora, or mountain slopes. Powerful butterflies will survive in forest or woodland canopies, living up at the treetops; weak fliers prefer to stay closer to the ground amongst shrubs and trees which will provide protection from winds. Butterflies found in woodland will often be coloured red, brown or grey, so they resemble dry leaves or bark; others are bright green, like fresh leaves. Butterflies are dependent upon these particular places, and the loss of native habitats can only have dire consequences for their numbers.

Opposite: A fully emerged Monarch. The loss of their native habitat has a major impact on the survival of some butterfly species. Many will only feed on one particular plant or have adapted so successfully that they cannot survive in an alternative area.

Survival

With so many potential predators, butterflies and moths employ a number of techniques to aid survival. Many species are inedible; their caterpillars feed from host plants that contain poisons, storing these in their bodies so that the adult butterfly can benefit from the chemicals: the members of the Heliconius sub-family contain the poisons found in the larval food plant, passionflower (*passiflora*). Poisonous butterflies advertise this fact to birds, lizards and other insects with their brightly coloured and patterned wings. Many edible butterflies take advantage of these poisonous species by copying their appearance; this technique is known as mimicry. Butterflies will mimic others for one of two reasons: either to appear to be poisonous when not, as does the non-poisonous mimic of the Monarch, the Viceroy, or to emphasize their own poisonous status.

Edible species that do not mimic use other tactics. Many will adopt camouflage as an effective technique to avoid becoming prey; the Indian Leaf butterfly is an excellent example of this, as are a number of moths, including the Brindled Beauty. Others will use their wing markings to confuse or frighten

Above: Nymph butterfly on flowers.
Opposite: Some butterflies and moths, such as this Polyphemus moth (Antherea polyphemus), are well camouflaged so it can be difficult for them to find a mate by sight. For this reason, many species rely on their pheromones, or carry out elaborate courtship displays.

predators. Distinctive markings can suggest an even larger predator is at hand; the owl face seen by the enemy is simply the wings of the Owl Butterfly, the snake's head among the leaves is actually the hooked forewing of the Atlas moth. Eyespots are a particularly effective way of confusing and warding off enemies; some butterflies, such as the Blue Morpho, have a solid colour on their upper-side but large eyespots from below which startle a predator when they are flashed unexpectedly. Butterflies that use eyespots to frighten their enemies, such as the Peacock, can often find themselves with ragged wings as a result of inquisitive pecks from confused birds. Although dangerous, these pecks warn the Peacock of danger, giving it time to fly away.

PAPILIONIDAE
SWALLOWTAILS

PIPEVINE SWALLOWTAIL BATTUS PHILENOR

CATERPILLAR: Ruddy brown body with a line of red or black tentactles along the back. Feeds mainly on pipevines, but will eat other plants

WINGSPAN: 7–11cm

HABITAT: Meadows, riversides, urban gardens and roadsides; mountainous forest in the east, desert in the west

RANGE: Central states of North America down towards Central America

STATUS: More common further south

Swallowtails are so called because of the 'tails' that emerge from their hindwings. The Pipevine Swallowtail has broad, pointed forewings and rounded hindwings with gentle scallops and short tails. The forewings are a dull, blackish colour and the hindwings are an iridescent blue with pale creamy markings on the upper side. The underside of the hindwings is blue, marked with a row of seven large, black-ringed orange spots. Females are duller and lack the blue sheen seen on the males. The caterpillar's almost exclusive diet of pipevine leaves makes both it and the adult butterfly poisonous, and as a result the butterfly is the model for mimics such as the Tiger Swallowtail.

BATTUS POLYDAMUS POLYDAMUS SWALLOWTAIL

Sometimes called the Tailless Polydamus, the Polydamus Swallowtail occurs in a number of regional forms but all members of this species share some key features. It has scalloped hindwings with no tails; its background colour is dark, almost black, often with a green sheen on the hindwings. There is a bright yellow band on each wing and yellow edges to the hindwings. The underside of the hindwing is marked with red spots or crescents, and its black body can often be spotted with red. The caterpillar feeds on poisonous plants, making both the pupa and the butterfly inedible for birds.

CATERPILLAR: Yellow body covered with fine black striping on each segment. Feeds on pipevines

WINGSPAN: 7–9cm

HABITAT: Open woodland, urban gardens and parks, forest canopies

RANGE: Southern states of North America down into Central and South America and the Caribbean

STATUS: Common and widespread, the Polydamus adapts well to different environments

BLUE TRIANGLE

GRAPHIUM SARPEDON

The Blue Triangle has long triangular forewings and relatively long, scalloped hindwings, but no tail. Its body and background colour are black; it has distinctive and striking bands of translucent blue-green across both wings, and these are marked with delicate black veins. There are also blue-green crescents marking the outer edges of the hindwings. Males have scent sacs on the inner edge of the hindwings which enable differentiation from the otherwise similar females.

CATERPILLAR: Green body with yellow stripes along its sides and short spines on the front and the back. Feeds on a variety of trees, including camphor, laurel and myrtle

WINGSPAN: 6–9cm

HABITAT: Open woodland, riverbanks, clearings and lowland forests

RANGE: From India to China and Japan, Malaysia and Australasia

STATUS: Common. In some areas the caterpillar is considered a pest

SCARCE SWALLOWTAIL IPHICLIDES PODALIRIUS

CATERPILLAR: Plump and green with yellow stripes, sometimes spotted red. Feeds on sloe and blackthorn

WINGSPAN: 7–9cm

HABITAT: Gardens, fields and open woodland

RANGE: Across central and southern Europe to China and Asia and north Africa

STATUS: Generally widespread and common; however in some areas of central Europe its habitat is under threat

Despite its name, the Scarce Swallowtail is a common sight in Europe. It has a creamy yellow background colour marked with striking dark bars. Some species have an almost white background colour with black stripes. The wedge-shaped stripes are wider towards the forewing, and the margins of both wings are lined with black. The hindwings are scalloped and have long streamers which are black with yellow edging. The scalloped margins are marked with blue spots and there is a red-orange and blue eyespot on the inner edge of the hindwing. They can easily be observed feeding on flowers, often lavender, with a floating, smooth flight.

PAPILIO CRESPHONTES GIANT SWALLOWTAIL

This black and yellow swallowtail is one of the largest butterflies that inhabits North America and is found particularly in the southern states, where its caterpillars are considered to be a pest in areas where citrus fruit is grown. The butterfly can be distinguished by the diagonal band of yellow spots on each forewing. Large yellow spots also line the margins of each wing and there are yellow eyespots on the tails. Its background colour is black, as is its upper body; however its abdomen is yellow with a central black streak. Two small red and black eyespots mark the inner edge of each hindwing.

CATERPILLAR: Brown with irregular white marks. It feeds on wild plants, citrus and garden plants, and is considered a pest in orange groves

WINGSPAN: 10–15cm

HABITAT: Woodland, orchards, gardens and lowlands.

RANGE: Central America up to southern states of North America, particularly Florida and Texas

STATUS: Common in localized areas

TIGER SWALLOWTAIL PAPILIO GLAUCUS

CATERPILLAR: Leaf green and plump, the caterpillar is excellently camouflagued. Feeds on trees, particularly cherry, willow and ash

WINGSPAN: 9–17cm

HABITAT Woodland, wooded gardens and parks

RANGE: Across the North American continent, from Alaska and Canada to Mexico

STATUS: Widespread and common

The yellow- and black-striped appearance of this swallowtail has resulted in its popular name of 'tiger'. Its background colour is yellow with black stripes on the forewing and black wing margins lined with yellow spots. It has a black V-shaped marking on the hindwing, its tail streamers are black and its hindwing edges are gently scalloped. Its abdomen is black with yellow stripes, matching the wings. Males and females are generally similar; however in some more southern females the yellow markings are lacking, with some purely black examples. These darker butterflies are believed to be mimicking the highly poisonous Pipevine Swallowtail (*Battus philenor*).

PAPILIO MACHAON SWALLOWTAIL

Referred to as the 'Old World Swallowtail' in the United States, this butterfly is widespread across the temperate northern hemisphere. It has distinctive and easily recognized patterning and short, delicate tail streamers. The background colour of the wings is a creamy yellow which is marked with black veins. The outer margins of the forewings are lined with black, lined in turn with yellow spots. The marginal band on the hindwing is blue-black, with a red eyespot in each corner. This swallowtail is a particularly strong, fast flier.

CATERPILLAR: Bright green with black stripes spotted with red. Feeds on carrot, milkweed, dill and fennel

WINGSPAN: 8–10cm

HABITAT: Open grassland, swamps, fenland and damp meadows

RANGE: Across Europe to Asia and Japan; northern Africa; sub-Arctic North America

STATUS: Widespread and common

BLACK SWALLOWTAIL

PAPILIO POLYXENES

A common and widespread swallowtail, the Black Swallowtail, as its name suggests, is mainly black. It has a bright yellow band across both wings; yellow spots also line the margins of both wings. Females often show less yellow than the males with a narrower band. Both have an iridescent blue patch on each hindwing between the bands. It has a small red eyespot on the inner edge of each hindwing and its abdomen is black lined with yellow spots. Can usually be seen flying in the full sun, looking for flowers to feed on.

CATERPILLAR: Bright green with black stripes spotted with red. Feeds on carrot, milkweed, dill and fennel

WINGSPAN: 8–10cm

HABITAT: Open grassland, swamps, fenland and damp meadows

RANGE: Across Europe to Asia and Japan; northern Africa, sub-Arctic North America

STATUS: Widespread and common

APOLLO PARNASSIUS APOLLO

CATERPILLAR: Black with orange side spots. Feeds on sedum and houseleek

WINGSPAN: 6–10cm

HABITAT: Alpine meadows and mountain slopes; in the colder northern part of its range it keeps to lower altitudes

RANGE: European and Central Asian mountain ranges

STATUS: Generally common but highly sought after by collectors, therefore a protected species

This mountain butterfly is appropriately named after the mountain of the Greek gods, Parnassus. It has a white background colour and the forewings are edged with an iridescent grey. The forewings are marked with large black spots and the hindwings bear colour spots that can vary from red to orange and dark yellow. These distinctive spots distinguish the Apollo from similar species, such a the Small Apollo, which has a red spot on its forewing, or the Clouded Apollo, which bears no coloured spots. The abdomen of the Apollo is covered with relatively long grey hairs and its grey antennae have a black club.

ZERYNTHIA POLYXENA SOUTHERN FESTOON

This striking butterfly has delicate and intricate patterning, making it very distinctive. Its background colour is a creamy yellow and this is marked with a variable patterning of almost geometric black markings. The wing-edges are striped with black and cream crescents. It has a red patch on the leading edge of the forewing and several red spots on the hindwing. The Southern Festoon closely resembles the Spanish Festoon (*Zerynthia rumina*) which is more yellow and has a greater number of red patches on the forewing.

CATERPILLAR: Feeds on vines and birthwort

WINGSPAN: 5–6cm

HABITAT: Open grassland, agricultural land and vineyards

RANGE: Central and southern Europe across to Eurasia

STATUS: Common in localized areas; however its habitat is under threat in some places

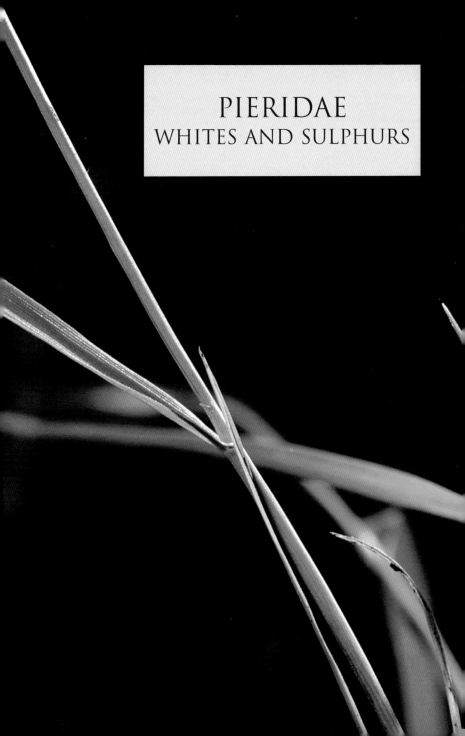

PIERIDAE
WHITES AND SULPHURS

BLACK-VEINED WHITE APORIA CRATAEGI

CATERPILLAR: Hairy grey body with a black back marked with red. Feeds on hawthorns and fruit trees such as peach, apple and pear

WINGSPAN: 6–8cm

HABITAT: Flowery meadows and roadsides, orchards and forest edges

RANGE: Across Europe, although extinct in Britain. Found in north Africa and Asia

STATUS: Common, particularly in orchards, where the larvae are considered pests

A striking white, the black veining on this butterfly makes it distinctive and easy to identify. Its white wings are almost translucent and the veins can appear dark brown to black. It has rounded wings and a large dark grey body with clubbed antennae. The edges of its wings are delicately lined with black; often grey scaling can be seen on the wing-edges and the underside, otherwise the upper side and underside are similar. Large numbers of these butterflies can often be observed together as they drink from puddles. As caterpillars they live communally in the cocoon.

LEPTIDEA SINAPIS WOOD WHITE

The Wood White is a small, delicate butterfly, with relatively broad rounded wings and a long, slender abdomen. It is a weak flier, often fluttering close to the ground and generally unable to tolerate winds; as a consequence it is usually observed fluttering through foliage rather than above. Its wings are pure white above, with a pale grey coloration at the outer tip of the forewing, a marking that is more pronounced in males. Its white underwing is slightly more yellow, with pale grey streaks along the veins. Its abdomen is grey.

CATERPILLAR: Pale green with a black back and yellow side stripes. Feeds on members of the pea family

WINGSPAN: 4–5cm

HABITAT: Mainly woodland, particularly sheltered areas

RANGE: Across Europe, from the British Isles into central Europe

STATUS: Restricted to areas with suitable habitat

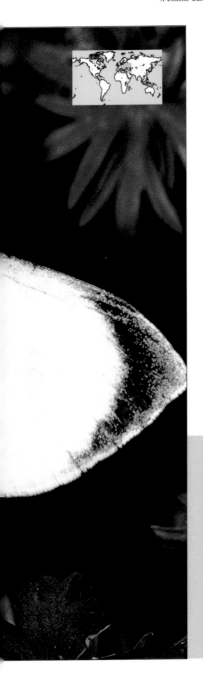

LARGE WHITE OR CABBAGE WHITE

PIERIS BRASSICAE

Commonly known as the Large Cabbage White, this common garden visitor can be distinguished from its smaller relative *Pieris rapae* by its slightly larger size and darker markings. Its wings are predominantly white on the upper side, with two dark spots and black tips on the leading edges of the forewings, markings that are generally darker on the female. Its underside is a greenish yellow with a white central patch on the forewing marked with a black spot. The butterfly is attracted to flowers, but its caterpillar is more infamous as a voracious eater of all members of the cabbage or brassica family.

CATERPILLAR: Green body with a black back bordered with yellow stripes. Feeds on cabbage, but also nasturtiums
WINGSPAN: 6cm
HABITAT: Meadows, agricultural land, parks and gardens
RANGE: Widespread across Europe into north Africa
STATUS: Common. Has been known to migrate into northern reaches of its range

GREEN VEINED WHITE PIERIS NAPI

CATERPILLAR: Bright green with fine yellow spots along the sides. Feeds on cress, mustard, garlic and watercress

WINGSPAN: 5cm

HABITAT: Damp meadows and woodland, gardens and roadside edges

RANGE: Widespread across Europe, from Scandinavia towards the Mediterranean

STATUS: Common

Whilst this may appear to be similar to its relatives the Small and Large Cabbage Whites, the Green-Veined White is most easily distinguished by its veining, particularly on its underwings. It has a background colour of white on its upper side, with grey-green veining and either one (males) or two (females) similarly coloured spots on the forewing. The forewing tip is marked with dark grey. On its underside the background colour is a creamy yellow and on the hindwing this is delicately patterned with grey-green veins. The underside of the forewing is more white but with a yellow tip, and the spots seen on the upperwing are repeated below.

PIERIS RAPAE SMALL WHITE

Like its close relative the *Pieris brassicae*, the Small White is best known for its caterpillars' attraction to cabbage, earning it the common name Small Cabbage White. It is particularly common and easily seen in almost every garden where flowering plants grow. Its upper side is mainly white, with dark grey edges to the tips of the forewings and and one grey spot on males, two on females. The hindwings are creamy white and also bear a grey spot, usually less distinct in males. The underside is a greyish yellow, with a whiter forewing but otherwise matching markings. Small whites are migratory and can often be observed in large groups or swarms.

CATERPILLAR: Small and pale green. Feeds on cabbage, radishes and nasturtiums

WINGSPAN: 4–5cm

HABITAT: Gardens, roadsides, meadows, uncultivated fields and argricultural land

RANGE: This is a widespread butterfly found in most suitable habitats around the world

STATUS: Extremely numerous and common

BATH WHITE

PONTIA DAPLIDICE

This strong, fast flier is a regular migrant and consequently covers a large range. Its background colour is white and on the upper side its wings are strongly marked with dark grey, almost black, patterning. On the forewing this is restricted to marks on the outer tip and a large squarish spot in the centre, whereas on the hindwing the spots are extensive, producing a marbled effect. From below, the same markings are repeated but in an olive green rather than black. This colouring helps to provide better camouflage when the butterfly is at rest within foliage. Females are slightly larger, with more marbling on the hindwing.

CATERPILLAR: Slender with a green body covered with black spots and yellow stripes along back and sides. Feeds on reseda and rock cress
WINGSPAN: 5cm
HABITAT: Open, flowery grassland and meadows, roadsides, gardens and parkland
RANGE: Across central and southern Europe, towards north Africa
STATUS: Particularly common towards the southern end of its range

ORANGE SULPHUR
COLIAS EURYTHEME

CATERPILLAR: Dark green body with white, black and pink side stripes. Feeds on alfafa, clover and other legumes

WINGSPAN: 4–6cm

HABITAT: Open fields, agricultural land, meadows and prairies

RANGE: Across North America

STATUS: More common in south and west; caterpillar is considered a pest in some areas

Found across North America, this species is commonly referred to as the Orange Sulphur, the Alfafa Caterpillar Butterfly or the Alfafa Sulphur. Its background colour can vary from bright yellow to a more orange colour; yellow examples can usually be seen during spring. Both males and females have a dark brown border across both wings. However, in the female this is incomplete, with patches of the background colour showing through. There is a black spot in the centre of the forewing, visible from below as a pale spot. An orange spot on the upper side of the hindwing is an identifying feature; this too is pale underneath. The background colour on the underside is yellow-green with a row of dark spots at the outer edge of each wing.

CLOUDED/COMMON SULPHUR
COLIAS PHILODICE

This common North American butterfly can display either clear yellow or yellow-white wings, but generally paler examples are females. Both males and females bear distinctive black outer margins on both wings and in the females this can be broken up with patches of the background wing colour. There is a single dark eyespot on the forewing and a single, paler brown spot on the hindwing. These markings show through on the solid-coloured underside, with the hindwing spot showing as white edged with black.

CATERPILLAR: Green and white striped body. Feeds on clover and alfalfa
WINGSPAN: 5–7cm
HABITAT: Open fields and agricultural land, roadside edges
RANGE: Across North America
STATUS: Generally common

CLOUDED YELLOW

COLIAS CROCEA

A native of southern Europe, this fast-flying butterfly is able to migrate long distances towards the north, extending its range substantially. The males are brighter than the females, with an upperwing background colour of orange-yellow broadly bordered with dark brown. The forewing bears a dark brown spot in its centre. On its underwing the male has an orange-yellow background colour with a green tinge to the forewing margin and the hindwing. It shows a dark spot on the forewing and a pale, ringed spot on the hindwing. Females are much less vivid and generally a more greenish yellow.

CATERPILLAR: Slender and pale green with white side stripes delicately spotted with red. Feeds on clover and sweet-peas
WINGSPAN: 5cm
HABITAT: Open grassland, meadows, agricultural land and wasteland
RANGE: Southern and central Europe, reaching as far north as Britain
STATUS: Common in its native habitat, less so further north

PALE CLOUDED YELLOW COLIAS HYALE

CATERPILLAR: Pale green with a white stripe along the side. Feeds on clover and alfalfa
WINGSPAN: 5cm
HABITA: Open lowland, particularly flowery grassland, meadows and agricultural fields
RANGE: Northern and central Europe
STATUS: Generally common in its range

This is similar in appearance to its relative the Clouded Yellow, but as its name suggests it is paler and shows no orange; this is the most usual feature by which to differentiate the two. The Pale Clouded Yellow also has a slightly more pointed forewing. Females are much paler than the males, but both are yellow, the males more vividly so. The forewing bears a central black spot and the hindwing has a pale spot ringed with reddish brown. The female's forewing is almost white, particularly from the underside. When at rest, it keeps its wings closed above its body.

GONEPTERYX CLEOPATRA CLEOPATRA

Similar in appearance to its relative the Brimstone, the Cleopatra inhabits a more southerly range and has more strikingly coloured upper wings. It is predominantly bright yellow above, with the centre of the forewing showing bright orange in the males. The hindwing bears a small orange-brown spot. Females are generally much paler. The underside is a pale green-yellow with a small ruddy brown spot in the centre of each wing. Its most distinguishing feature is the orange streak across the centre of the forewing on the underside. Again, females are much paler below, being almost white in colour. Both sexes have hooked forewing tips and angular hindwings, giving them a leaf-like appearance when at rest.

CATERPILLAR: Pale green with a fine white stripe along the sides. Feeds on buckthorn.
WINGSPAN: 6–7cm
HABITAT: Woodland edges, scrubland, open and lightly wooded lowland
RANGE: Mediterranean Europe down to north Africa
STATUS: Common in its chosen habitat

BRIMSTONE

GONEPTERYX RHAMNI

Aside from its interesting appearance, the Brimstone is also the butterfly credited with the invention of the common English term for all Lepidoptera: its yellow colouring originally earning it the name 'butter-coloured fly'. It is only the male Brimstone that is yellow on its upper side, however: females are a creamy white colour. On the underside, the male is a yellow-green colour and when its wings are folded at rest it takes on the appearance of a fresh leaf. Again the female is far paler on the underside; however, both bear a small brown spot on each wing. The hooked tip of the forewing and the angular shape of the hindwing contribute to its leaf-like appearance.

CATERPILLAR: Slender and pale green with a fine white stripe along the side. Feeds on buckthorn
WINGSPAN: 6cm
HABITAT: Woodland edges, flowery grassland, meadows, gardens and fenland
RANGE: Europe, from Britain down towards the Mediterranean
STATUS: Generally common

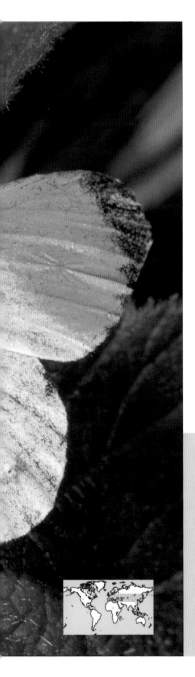

ORANGE TIP
ANTHOCHARIS CARDAMINES

Males and females in this species are quite
different, with the striking males being the
most easily recognized of the two. Both are
white butterflies; however the male has a
bright orange tip to the forewing which is
edged with brown and bears a small brown
central spot. The female has no orange, but
a broader brown tip and a larger central
spot on the forewing. Both have delicate,
olive-green mottled hindwings on the
underside, which helps to provide
camouflage when the butterfly is at rest.
Females are very similar to the slightly
darker female Bath Whites, and
consequently difficult to identify.

CATERPILLAR: Pale grey-green with white side stripes.
   Feeds on *Cardamine pratensis* and garlic mustard
WINGSPAN: 4–5cm
HABITAT: Light woodland, meadows and grassland,
   fenland and sometimes gardens
RANGE: Across Europe towards Asia
STATUS: Common

TIGER PIERID

DISMORPHIA AMPHIONE

Although this is a Pierid butterfly, the Tiger Pierid has an unusually long and narrow wing shape that more closely resembles that of the *Heliconius* butterflies. It is an effective mimic, with striking black, orange and yellow wings that suggest poisons to potential predators. The pattern of its markings can vary, but generally the forewing is backgrounded in black with orange patches from the base and yellow patches towards the tip. The dark hindwing has a large orange patch on females, and an orange streak accompanied by a translucent white patch on males.

CATERPILLAR: Dark green body. Feeds on *Inga sapindoides*
WINGSPAN: 4–4.5cm
HABITAT: Tropical forests
RANGE: South and central America, West Indies
STATUS: Generally common

ORANGE-BARRED GIANT SULPHUR

PHOEBIS PHILEA

As its common name suggests, this is a large sulphur with broad wings clearly marked with orange. The sexes are slightly different: males have shallower wings, which are solid yellow with a distinctive orange patch or bar on the forewing. The female has squared wings, also yellow but with dark brown edges and spotting on the forewing and a red blush to the edges of the hindwing. This red colouring includes a row of red-brown oval spots along the edge. From underneath, both sexes are a solid orange-yellow, darker in the female, and both show a dark-ringed white spot in the centre of each wing.

CATERPILLAR: Pale green body with brown side stripe. Feeds on senna
WINGSPAN: 7–8cm
HABITAT: Subtropical forest edges and clearings
RANGE: Southern states of the USA into Central America towards southern Brazil
STATUS: Generally common

LYCENIDAE
GOSSAMER WINGS

GREEN HAIRSTREAK CALLOPHRYS RUBI

CATERPILLAR: Green body with dark back and diagonal yellow stripes. Feeds on low-growing plants such as gorse and heather

WINGSPAN: 2.5cm

HABITAT: Scrubland, heaths, meadows, open grassland and woodland edges

RANGE: Across Europe into Asia and north Africa

STATUS: Generally common

On its upper side the Green Hairstreak is a fairly dull brown colour; its veins are slightly darker than the background colour, and males show a small pale scent patch near the leading edge of the forewing. It is the underside of the butterfly that earns it the common name, as both wings are a bright, leafy green. On the hindwing there is a broken white band, which continues on to the forewing, but only faintly. Its slightly scalloped hindwing is fringed with white and brown. When at rest, the Green Hairstreak keeps its wings closed, making it extremely difficult to spot in foliage.

EUMAEUS ATALA ATALA

Although considered a hairstreak, the Atala lacks any tails, nor indeed are its hindwings scalloped. It is a striking butterfly, with black wings washed with iridescent blue-green scales. The hindwing bears a single row of metallic-blue spots along the marginal edge on the upper side, and from below there are three rows of the same markings. The bright red abdomen and red hindwing spot are distinctive and enable identification. The thorax and head of the butterfly are black with faint blue spotting. Virtually extinct in the United States, the Atala has been successfully reintroduced.

CATERPILLAR: Red body with yellow spotting. Feeds on zamia
WINGSPAN: 4–5cm
HABITAT: Tropical and subtropical forests, parks and gardens
RANGE: Central America, Cuba, the Bahamas into Florida
STATUS: Increasingly common

PURPLE HAIRSTREAK

QUERCUSIA QUERCUS

When at rest, this hairstreak will sometimes leave its wings open, allowing observers to identify it by the markings on its upperwings. These have a sooty brown background colour with bright patches of iridescent purple. On the male, the purple covers almost all of both wings, leaving the brown at the outer margins, whereas the females show purple only on a patch at the centre of the forewing. The underside of both sexes is a pale silvery grey with a single white streak along the outer edge and small orange spots on the tip of the hindwing. There is a very small tail on the hindwing.

CATERPILLAR: Ruddy brown body with dark brown markings. Feeds on oak trees
WINGSPAN: 2–3cm
HABITAT: Mainly deciduous woodland, particulary those containing oak
RANGE: Across Europe into Asia and towards north Africa
STATUS: Generally common

GREY HAIRSTREAK
STRYMON MELINUS

CATERPILLAR: Green with white markings along its side. Feeds on a variey of plants, including cotton, maize and hops, resulting in its being considered a pest

WINGSPAN: 2–3cm

HABITAT: Open land, fields, meadows gardens, roadside verges and forest edges.

RANGE: From Canada, through to Central and South America

STATUS: Widespread and very common

This is one of the most common and widespread hairstreaks in North America. The larva of the Grey Hairstreak feeds on a wide variety of plants, allowing it to prosper in a range of habitats. From above the male is dark grey and bears an orange and black eyespot above the tail on the hindwing. Females are a more brownish grey. On its underside, the Grey Hairstreak is silvery grey with a delicate orange, black and white band crossing the wings. Its orange and black eyespot can be seen from the underside. Its body and abdomen correspond with the wing coloration, dark above, paler below.

WHITE LETTER HAIRSTREAK
STRYMONIDIA W-ALBUM

At first glance this is simply a dull brown hairstreak, but the white markings on both underside wings are distinctive and enable a clear identification. From above it has dark, chocolate-brown wings with gentle scalloping and two short tails on the hindwing. On the underside the wings are a slightly paler brown, with a clear W-shaped white streak across both wings. At the outer margin of the hindwing are a number of crescent-shaped orange patches forming a bright band. The upper side of the wings is rarely seen when the butterfly is at rest.

CATERPILLAR: Pale green body with pinkish diagonal streaks and dark green back stripes. Feeds on elm

WINGSPAN: 3–4cm

HABITAT: Deciduous woodland, woodland edges and hedgerows

RANGE: Across Europe into Asia

STATUS: Generally common, but numbers affected by Dutch elm disease

BROWN HAIRSTREAK THECLA BETULAE

CATERPILLAR: Green with yellow stripes. Feeds on blackthorn
WINGSPAN: 3–4cm
HABITAT: Woodland edges, hedgerows and scrubland
RANGE: Across Europe into Asia
STATUS: Relatively common within chosen habitat, where small colonies are formed

From above, as its names suggests, the Brown Hairstreak is mainly brown in colour, with orange patches on the forewing which are larger in the female than the male. Both sexes also bear an orange mark on the small tail. From below the Brown Hairstreak is more remarkable, with a subtle orange background colour marked with two delicate black and white lines on each wing. The tail streamer is a brighter orange from below. Its body shows dark brown from above and paler below.

LYCAENA DISPAR LARGE COPPER

Despite its small size, the Large Copper is relatively big in comparison to other coppers. Males have upperwings that are a bright coppery orange, clearly bordered with dark brown and bearing a small brown spot in the centre of the forewing. Females are less bright, with a greater amount of dark brown, a broader brown border on the forewing and dull brown hindwings; they also bear a number of brown spots along the length of the forewing. On the underside, the sexes are similar, with an orange forewing bearing dark spots and a bright, blue-grey hindwing with black spots and an orange band.

CATERPILLAR: Bright green with raised white spots. Feeds on water dock and varieties of aquatic sorrel

WINGSPAN: 3–4cm

HABITAT: Damp grassland, marshes, fenland and the banks of slow-flowing rivers

RANGE: Localized from eastern Britain, into northern and central Europe.

STATUS: Numbers are in decline due to degradation of habitat

SMALL COPPER

LYCAENA PHLAEAS

This species of copper has a wide range, mainly thanks to its host plant, sorrel, which grows in abundance in the warm and temperate parts of the globe. Males and females are similar, with bright orange forewings bordered with brown and bearing black spots. The hindwings are greyish brown with an orange border marked with brown spots. The underwings are similarly marked but the colours are less bright. It has a dark body and long antennae ringed in black and white.

CATERPILLAR: Green with purple and pink markings. Feeds on sorrel and dock
WINGSPAN: 2–3cm
HABITAT: Open grassland, fields, meadows and roadsides
RANGE: Found across temperate northern hemisphere
STATUS: Widespread and extremely common

SOOTY COPPER LYCAENA TITYRUS

CATERPILLAR: Plump, green body. Feeds on dock and sorrel
WINGSPAN: 3–4cm
HABITAT: Open grassland, flowery meadows, low-lying mountain slopes, coastal fields
RANGE: Across Europe but not Britain or Scandinavia
STATUS: Generally common

It is the male that is more 'sooty' in appearance, with upperwings that are a dark blackish brown with black spots on both wings. On the hindwing marginal edge there is a series of orange spots making an irregular line. The female is slightly more colourful, with orange forewings marked with black spots and a much more defined orange band around the hindwing edge. From below its wings are a paler grey, with the black markings showing through and a row of orange spots along the edge of both wings.

ARICIA AGESTIS BROWN ARGUS

This attractive little brown butterfly can be identified by the distinctive orange spots along its wing margins. Its upperwings are a rich brown colour and the bright orange spots are highlighted with black on the hindwings. The forewing has a single black spot at its centre. The slightly larger females have proportionally bigger spot markings. From underneath, the pale grey-brown wings are marked with white-ringed black spots. The orange spots are repeated from the upper side, with the black highlights on the hindwing ringed in white. In addition, a white streak marks the centre of the hindwing. The white wing fringe is visible on both sides.

CATERPILLAR: Green body with purple and dark green stripes. Feeds on rock rose and cranesbill
WINGSPAN: 2.5cm
HABITAT: Open grassland and heaths
RANGE: Temperate northern Europe
STATUS: Generally common

HOLLY BLUE CELASTRINA ARGIOLUS

CATERPILLAR: Pale green
with pink stripes along
the sides and back.
Feeds on holly and ivy
WINGSPAN: 2–3cm
HABITAT: Mainly woodland
but also parks and
gardens, wherever host
plants can be found
RANGE: Across Europe,
down to north Africa
and through to Asia
STATUS: Generally common
and widespread

A fairly frequent garden visitor, the Holly Blue is an
easily identified member of the blues. It is particularly
attracted to those gardens where holly and ivy are
grown, since it uses both these plants to host its larva.
Both males and females have blue upperwings; however
the female is more pale and dull and shows a greater
amount of brownish black on the wing margins. The
male is a bright violet blue, with a narrow black margin
at the forewing tip. Both have a short white fringe which
is intermittently marked with black. The pale silvery-
blue underwings are marked with small black spots.

EVERES COMYNTAS EASTERN TAILED BLUE

This species of common blue has, as its name suggests, a fine hair-like tail on its hindwings. In coloration males and females differ: males are deep blue from above with a narrow black border; females are a dark grey, often shot with blue. Both sexes bear a pair of orange and black eyespots on the tail end of the hindwing. From below, both are a dirty white marked with dark grey spots in a curving line. The eyespots are visible on the underwing.

CATERPILLAR: Green with brown and paler green stripes. Feeds on clover

WINGSPAN: 2cm

HABITAT: Open grassland, meadows, fields, roadsides and large, lawned gardens

RANGE: South-eastern Canada, eastern states of North America into Central America

STATUS: Common

LONG-TAILED BLUE LAMPIDES BOETICUS

CATERPILLAR: Pale green body with darker green back stripe and pale diagonal stripes. Feeds on pea plants
WINGSPAN: 3.5cm
HABITAT: Open grassland, meadows, heathland
RANGE: Mediterranean Europe into north Africa
STATUS: Generally common within its native range

This migratory butterfly is native to the south of Europe, but will often succeed in making its way as far north as southern England. It has fairly pointed forewings and squarer hindwings with a distinctive tail, not dissimilar to that of a typical hairstreak. However the Long-tailed Blue's colouring is distinctive. Males are a solid violet-blue on the upper side with a white patch bearing two black eyespots above the tail; females are more brown from above, with violet-blue showing at the base of the wings. From below, both sexes are much paler brown, with buff and white streaks and bars across both wings and the eyespots boldly repeated.

MACULINEA ARION LARGE BLUE

As a member of the Maculinea genus, the Large Blue's caterpillars rely upon the eggs of red ants in order to pupate. Young caterpillars allow themselves to be carried into the nest by the ants; they then gorge themselves on the grubs, leaving the nest after pupation as a fresh butterfly. Males and females are both blue from above, although the female shows deep brown wing margins. Both sexes bear black marks on the upper forewing. The underside is a grey-brown patterned with brown spots ringed with white. Females tend to be slightly larger than males.

CATERPILLAR: Creamy white body. Feeds on thyme and marjoram plants then ant eggs and larvae

WINGSPAN: 3–4cm

HABITAT: Dry, chalky grassland, wherever caterpillar food sources are present

RANGE: Europe, excluding Britain, into Asia and China

STATUS: Widespread but scarce and declining

ADONIS BLUE

LYSANDRA BELLARGUS

The males of the Adonis Blue species are a
particularly striking bright blue colour from
above, and their wings are fringed with a
white and black chequered border. The
female is a rich brown colour above, with
blue scales producing a subtle sheen. At the
base of the female's hindwings there is a
border of crescent-shaped orange spots.
Both sexes have grey-brown underwings
which are marked with black spots and a
border of orange and black on each wing.

CATERPILLAR: Green body with yellow stripes. Feeds on
horseshoe vetch
WINGSPAN: 3–4cm
HABITAT: Dry, open grassland and meadows
RANGE: From western Europe into Asia
STATUS: Generally common, but numbers slowly being
affected by habitat loss

ACMON BLUE PLEBEJUS ACMON

CATERPILLAR: Yellow-green body with dark green back stripe and white hairs. Feeds on legumes and buckwheat foliage
WINGSPAN: 2.5–3cm
HABITAT: Open, dry fields, wasteland, agricultural land, meadows
RANGE: Across North America, from southern Canada towards Mexico
STATUS: Generally common

This North American blue can most easily be identified by the band of orange spots that lines the hindwing. As is typical, it is the male butterfly that is blue on the upper side; the female is a rich brown colour with the merest suggestion of blue at the wing base. The edges of both wings are dark blue-black, which contrasts strongly with the white fringe. The hindwing spots are black on a base of orange. These orange and black spots are repeated on the underside of the wing, which is a pale grey colour and which also bears simple black spotting.

PLEBEJUS ARGUS SILVER STUDDED BLUE

This is a particularly active and fast-flying blue, which tends to rest only early or late in the day. Males are a deep azure blue bordered with brown and then deep white wing-edges and fringe. The upperwings of the female are mainly brown with a crescent of orange marginal spots on the hindwing. Both sexes have pale grey underwings, which are marked with black spots, those on the hindwing having a slightly green hue. Both underwings bear a marginal line of orange spots. Its hairy body is blue-grey above and paler below.

CATERPILLAR: Green body with white side stripes and a black back. Feeds on heather and gorse. In some areas the larvae pupate inside ants' nests

WINGSPAN: 2–3cm

HABITAT: Heathland, hillside meadows, low mountain grassland and dunes

RANGE: Across Europe into Asia towards Japan

STATUS: Common and widespread

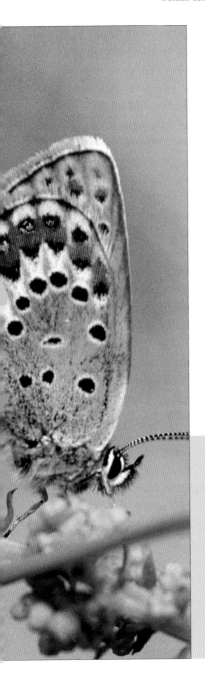

IDAS BLUE

PLEBEJUS IDAS

A small, attractive blue with dissimilar
males and females. Typical males have
violet-blue upperwings with a fine black
margin and a hairy white fringe. The
upperwing of the female is a rich brown
colour. Their underwings are similar, with a
background colour of pale grey-brown
marked with black spots and an orange band
of spots curving parallel to the outer
margins.

CATERPILLAR: Pale green back bordered with white
stripes and black sides. Feeds on members of the pea
family
WINGSPAN: 3cm
HABITAT: Open grassland, meadows, fields and
agricultural land
RANGE: Across northern and central Europe, including
higher altitudes
STATUS: Common

COMMON BLUE
POLYOMMATUS ICARUS

CATERPILLAR: Green body with pale green markings. Feeds on bird's-foot trefoil
WINGSPAN: 3–4cm
HABITAT: Open grassland, including higher altitude meadows
RANGE: Across Europe into Asia and north Africa
STATUS: Widespread and common

A typical blue butterfly, the Common Blue is also, as its name suggests, the blue butterfly most often observed in the field. The male has bright violet-blue upperwings with a delicate brown border and white fringe along the outer edges. The female has upperwings that are a solid rich brown colour with orange spots and crescents along the outer margins of both wings. Across some areas females will also show a blue wash to the inner base of the wings. Both sexes have similar undersides, which are pale grey-brown marked with black white-ringed spots and a marginal border of orange spots.

DUKE OF BURGUNDY FRITILLARY
HAMEARIS LUCINA

Although its name suggests otherwise, the Duke of Burgundy belongs not to the Nymphalidae species of fritillaries, but to the Riodinidae. It is the only metalmark butterfly native to Europe, and although it bears a strong resemblance to other fritillaries its behaviour is closer to that of the blues. From above, its deep brown wings are marked with a chequered pattern of orange spots and its fringe is chequered white and brown. It is orange-brown below, with dark spots on the forewing and broad white markings on the hindwing. The sexes are generally alike, but the female is slightly brighter and has more rounded forewings.

CATERPILLAR: Brown body with a dark stripe along the back. Feeds on primrose and cowslip
WINGSPAN: 3–4cm
HABITAT: Woodland edges, meadows and gardens
RANGE: Western and central Europe
STATUS: Generally common in local areas

NYMPHALIDAE
BRUSHFOOTS

WHITE PEACOCK

ANARTIA JATROPHAE

A common butterfly to Central and South America and the West Indies, the White Peacock is an attractive grey-white colour marked with bands of brown which create a chequered pattern. The wing margins are bordered with brown-orange crescents and the wings are gently scalloped, more so on the hindwing, which has a short tail. There are two dark eyespots on the hindwing and one on the forewing, and these are visible from below. The underside is much paler, showing more white, but with the pattern reproduced in pale orange and brown. Males and females are similar.

Caterpillar: Black body with black spines and silver spots. Feeds on water hyssop
Wingspan: 5–6cm
Habitat: Open land, fields, wasteland, gardens and roadsides
Range: Central and South America, West Indies and southern states of North America
Status: Common and widespread

PURPLE EMPEROR APATURA IRIS

CATERPILLAR: Plump, pale green body. Feeds on willow

WINGSPAN: 6–8cm

HABITAT: Deciduous woodland, particularly those with mature oaks, the tops of which are the preferred territory for males

RANGE: From western Europe into central Asia

STATUS: Generally common, but difficult to observe in the forest canopy

At first sight a Purple Emperor may not appear to be purple at all; it is only when caught in the right light that males flash their colours. Males and females bear similar markings and both appear to have a background colour of brown on their upperwings. However, males have wing scales that are sensitive to light, producing bright purple. This is bordered on both wings with blackish brown and marked with a white bar across the hindwing which breaks up into spots on the forewing. There is a large purple, black and orange spot on the hindwing. From below both sexes are brown with white patches on both wings and a large purple, black and orange eyespot on the forewing. The smaller spot on the hindwing shows through on the underwing.

ASTEROCAMPA CELTIS HACKBERRY BUTTERFLY

It is the caterpillar of this species which feeds upon hackberry bushes; the butterfly can more usually be seen feeding from tree sap or animal droppings. The Hackberry Butterfly has tawny-brown wings with white spotting on the forewing tips and dark spots on the hindwing. The upper side of the forewing has a distinctive black spot on the outer edge and there is a series of black spots along the margin of the hindwing. From underneath the Hackberry has a paler background colour, with similar white-ringed eyespotting on the hindwing.

CATERPILLAR: Green body with yellow stripes. Feeds on hackberry
WINGSPAN: 4–5.5cm
HABITAT: A variety, including river woodland, desert canyon and urban parks
RANGE: Across North America
STATUS: Widespread and common

THE VICEROY

BASILARCHIA ARCHIPPUS

The Viceroy is an effective mimic of the more poisonous Monarch butterfly. Although it is edible for predators, it is still a successfully common and widespread butterfly across North America. Like the Monarch's, its upperwings have a background colour of orange which is boldly patterned with black wing veins and black borders marked with small white spots. However it has an additional black line running across its hindwing, a feature that is repeated on its underside. From below its wings are paler; the hindwing has a background colour of pale, pinkish orange and the forewing is pale orange with a central darker orange patch.

CATERPILLAR: Olive-green and brown body with bristles behind the head. Feeds on decidous trees, particularly willow
WINGSPAN: 7–7.5cm
HABITAT: Open, damp areas, river edges, streams, marshes
RANGE: Widespread from Canada down into Mexico
STATUS: Generally common

RED LACEWING

CETHOSIA BIBLIS

The Latin name for the Red Lacewing reflects the patterning on the underside of the wings, which can look like writing in a book (*biblios*). This poisonous butterfly has a background colour of rich ruddy brown below, with a delicate pattern of white and black lines. From above, males and females are different: the males are brighter, with an orange-red background colour, broad brown borders on the outer wing-edges and white V-shaped markings along the margins. Females are either much more brown above, or an olive-green colour, with similar white markings. Both sexes have scalloped wings.

CATERPILLAR: Poisonous spined body. Feeds on passionflowers
WINGSPAN: 8–9cm
HABITAT: Forest edges and clearings
RANGE: India and Pakistan across to China, Malaysia and Indonesia
STATUS: Generally common

OWL BUTTERFLY CALIGO IDOMENEUS

CATERPILLAR: Brown body with a forked tail. Feeds on banana leaves and is considered a pest on plantations
WINGSPAN: 12–15cm
HABITAT: Tropical forests and suitable agricultural land
RANGE: Found throughout South America
STATUS: Common and widespread

Caligo idomeneus is an example of a genus of South American butterflies which are large and marked with enormous owl-like eyespots. Its upper side is a rich dark brown shot through with purple-blue iridescence. There is a white diagonal line running down the forewing which diffuses into pale blue on the darker brown hindwing. The underside is patterned with fine brown and white feathered lines and the forewing edge has a slender brown border. There are two small eyespots in the outer tip of the forewing but the hindwing is marked with two larger eyespots, that in the centre of the hindwing being bigger and more startling for potential predators. Although diurnal, these butterflies, like owls, fly during the early hours and at dusk.

CHARAXES JASIUS TWO-TAILED PASHA

The Two-tailed Pasha is the only double-tailed butterfly found in Europe. It has angular wings with gently scalloped hindwings leading to two significant tails. On the upper side the wings are brown, with pale orange borders and subtle blue spots at the base of the tails. On its underside there is a delicate and intricate pattern of white lines with a broad white band running down both fore- and hindwing. Between the white lines it is coloured with black, brown, orange and purple-grey. It is also distinguished by being one of the largest members of the Nympalidae family, and by its tendency to gorge itself on the juice of rotten fruit, rendering it too intoxicated to fly.

CATERPILLAR: Green with white spots. Feeds on strawberry trees

WINGSPAN: 7–8cm

HABITAT: Orchards, woodland and forests, scrubland

RANGE: Mediterranean Europe down towards north Africa

STATUS: Generally locally common

PAINTED LADY

CYNTHIA CARDUI

This is a strong migratory butterfly, whose caterpillars are content to consume a wide variety of plants; consequently it can successfully survive almost anywhere. Its upperwings are patterned with orange and black, with white spots on the the forewing. The gentle scalloped hindwings are edged with black and there are four black spots lining the outer margin. On the underside it is much paler, with the forewing repeating the upperside pattern and the hindwing marbled in white-brown and pinks. The four distinguishing spots are repeated below and ringed with orange and black.

CATERPILLAR: Black with white spots and black or yellow spines. Prefers to feed on thistle and nettle, but will eat many other plants
WINGSPAN: 5–6cm
HABITAT: Most open land with plentiful flowers. Regularly visits gardens
RANGE: Widespread across the world, native to warm southern climes
STATUS: Very common

BALTIMORE

EUPHYDRYAS PHAETON

This largely black butterfly is marked with distinctive white and orange spotting on its upper side, which greatly aids identification. Observation is also helped by the fact that the Baltimore Checkerspot uses the widespread plantain as a larval host plant. From above its black wings are bordered with orange spots, with smaller white spotting towards the centre. A pair of orange spots mark the forewing leading edge and a single spot is seen at the centre of the hindwing. From below it is marked with black and white checkering, and a less prominent orange band on the outer edges. It is named after the design of the heraldic shield of the first Lord Baltimore, a seventeenth-century colonist.

CATERPILLAR: Black body with orange side stripe and black spines. Feeds on turtlehead, white ash and plantain
WINGSPAN: 4–6.5cm
HABITAT: Wet meadows and grassland, sphagnum bogs and drier hillsides
RANGE: Throughout eastern states of the US, from Nova Scotia
STATUS: Generally common

PEACOCK INACHIS IO

CATERPILLAR: Black and spiny body. Feeds in large colonies on nettle and hop
WINGSPAN: 5–6cm
HABITAT: Grassy meadows, fields and open land, parks and gardens. Particularly attracted to buddleia
RANGE: Across Europe into cooler parts of Asia and Japan
STATUS: Widespread and very common

From below the Peacock is a dull, mottled brown with untidily scalloped wing-edges, which provides good leaf camouflage. On its upperside it is mainly bright red with black edges lined with brown. It has a large eyespot on the tip of the forewing that is red, yellow and blue ringed with black. There is also a pair of smaller, pure white spots on the outer margins of the forewing. The large eyespot on the hindwing is blue and black ringed with creamy white. On the inner half of the leading edge of the forewing there is a narrow band of fine yellow and black stripes. Birds, confused by the bold eyespots, will often launch a peck at the wings of the Peacock. This has the effect of alerting the butterfly to the danger and tends to leave many of this species with ragged, damaged wings.

JUNONIA COENIA BUCKEYE

Male Buckeyes are notoriously territorial and will patrol their chosen space seeking out both mates and intruders. As a result they cover wide areas, travelling north during the summer months as they look for territory. They are brown-coloured from above with a pair of orange bars on the leading edge of the forewing. The most distinctive features are the large black eyespots ringed with orange, white and black – one on the forewing and two on the hindwing. The underside is grey-brown with similar bars but no eyespot.

CATERPILLAR: Dark olive-green with yellow and orange marks. Feeds on plantains
WINGSPAN: 5–6cm
HABITAT: Open sunny fields, grassland and shorelines
RANGE: Across North America, from Canada to Mexico
STATUS: Common and widespread

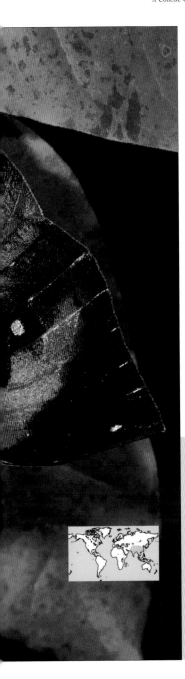

INDIAN LEAF BUTTERFLY

KALLIMA INACHUS

This butterfly earns its common name from the impressive camouflage patterning of its underside and for the shape of its wings, which closely resemble leaves. When at rest its underwings show brown, with paler vein markings and a single white 'mould' spot in the centre of the forewing. There is a line across both wings that resembles the spine of a leaf, and the hindwing tails closely resemble a leaf's stem. The wings themselves are angular with pointed forewing tips. The upper-side is much brighter: the forewings are broadly striped with brown, orange and blue, and the hindwings are brown with an iridescent blue wash. The Indian Leaf Butterfly is a particularly strong, rapid flier.

CATERPILLAR: Black body with red spines and yellow hairs. Feeds on girardinia and strobilanthus
WINGSPAN: 9–12cm
HABITAT: Rainforests, forest riverbanks
RANGE: From India and Pakistan across to China
STATUS: Generally common

WHITE ADMIRAL
LADOGA CAMILLA

CATERPILLAR: Brown body with green back and brown spines which extend on to the head. Feeds on honeysuckle

WINGSPAN: 5–6cm

HABITAT: Sunny clearings in mature woodland

RANGE: Western Europe, including southern England, across to central Asia and Japan

STATUS: Common, but not always easy to observe

The White Admiral is a rich black colour from above with bold white bands crossing the hindwing into the centre of the forewing. The forewing also bears large white spots at the outer tip. The round and gently scalloped hindwing is edged with fine crescents of white. All of these white markings are repeated on the underside of the butterfly; however there are additional white and black spots present on both the forewing and the hindwing and all of these are set against a background colour of orange-brown. The base of the underside hindwings is blue-grey, which extends into the colour of the body and abdomen.

SOUTHERN SNOUT BUTTERFLY
LIBYTHEANA CARINENTA

The Southern or American Snout Butterfly has an unusual appearance on two counts: its forewing tips are squared off, and it has a long 'nose' or snout-like protuberance from its face. Its wings from above are a black-brown colour with orange patches at the bases and white patches at the forewing tips. From below, its forewings match the upper side, while the hindwings are pale, mottled grey and brown, resembling a dry leaf. This migratory butterfly can appear in huge numbers in the southern part of its range, with swarms often exceeding the million mark.

CATERPILLAR: Dark green body with yellow stripes. Feeds on hackberry

WINGSPAN: 4–5cm

HABITAT: Woodland, edges and clearings, open fields and agricultural land

RANGE: Southern states of the USA into Central America

STATUS: More common in south-western states, generally numerous

BLUE MORPHO

MORPHO MENELAUS

The morphos are a sub-family of beautiful iridescent-blue butterflies that inhabit the rainforests of South America. The Morpho Peleides, commonly known as the Blue Morpho or the Common Morpho, is a striking example. From above it has striking iridescent blue wings broadly edged on the outer margins by deep brown-black. The dark forewing tips bear small white spots and both wings are gently scalloped. From below it is brown-edged with a series of fine white and cream lines. It has large black- and yellow-ringed eyespots, four on the hindwing, three on the fore, and these are used to confuse and deter predators. These strong, fast fliers are attracted to fermenting fruit.

CATERPILLAR: Striped red, brown and black with yellow back patches and red and brown hair tufts. When threatened it emits a strong scent. Feeds on pea plants

WINGSPAN: 9–12cm

HABITAT: Rainforest

RANGE: Central and South America and the West Indies

STATUS: Generally common, but threatened by both collectors and habitat loss

MALACHITE METAMORPHA STELENES

CATERPILLAR: Black with red spines. Feeds on ruellia and acanthus
WINGSPAN: 7–9cm
HABITAT: Subtropical forests, orchards, low mountain slopes, plantations
RANGE: South and Central America up into Florida, Jamaica and Cuba
STATUS: Very common

The semi-precious mineral malachite is a rich green colour, and the Malachite Butterfly has wings that are backgrounded with black and then patterned with bright green or yellowy-green patches. On the upper side, the green markings appear as a broad diagonal band across both wings from the base, with broken patches at the forewing tips. The hindwings, which are scalloped and slightly tailed, have a broken band of green patches along the marginal edge. From below the background colour is much paler light brown with olive markings. Females are larger and have paler wings.

NEPTIS SAPPHO COMMON GLIDER

The Common Glider earns it name for its unusual flight behaviour: it will often hold its wings out horizontally and glide. This gives observers a good opportunity to appreciate its striking wing patterning of black and white patches and stripes. Its wings have a background colour of black, and the forewings are marked with a diagonal stripe extending from the base and a series of patches forming a broken marginal band. The hindwing has a double band of white patches. From below it is a more brown colour and the repeated markings are creamy yellow. Most glider butterflies are found in west Africa or south-east Asia, but this species is unique to Europe.

CATERPILLAR: Feeds on pea plants
WINGSPAN: 4.5–5cm
HABITAT: Deciduous woodland, open scrubland, forest steppes
RANGE: From eastern Europe, into Russia towards Japan
STATUS: Locally common

CARDINAL PANDORIANA PANDORA

CATERPILLAR: Black body with orange stripes and spines. Feeds nocturnally on violets
WINGSPAN: 6–8cm
HABITAT: Woodland edges and clearings
RANGE: Southern Europe into north Africa and Asia
STATUS: Locally common

This European fritillary has an attractive combination of colours on its wings, which distinguishes it from its close relatives. On the upper side the wings are pale orange with black markings, including a band of diamond-shaped spots along the marginal edges of both wings. Spreading out from the base of the wings is a suffusion of pale green scales. On the underside this green is repeated in the background colour of the hindwings, which are also marked with delicate white bands, crescents and dots. The forewing tips are also pale green, while the remainder of the wing is a rosy pink with black spots.

PARTHENOS SYLVIA CLIPPER

This relatively large, broad-winged butterfly is a strong, swift flier. It has dark brown to orange-brown coloured wings, bearing variable patterns of paler brown stripes, crescents and patches and a number of translucent white patches on the forewing edges and tips. The underside of the wings tends to be similarly patterned, but paler than above, and its body is ringed with dark brown and orange. Rather confusingly, across some areas in its range there are varieties of Clipper with dark blue and green background colours; however, the white patches on the forewings are a clear identifying feature. The Clipper can often be observed basking along stream edges in large numbers.

CATERPILLAR: Olive-green with purple spines. Feeds on adenia
WINGSPAN: 10–11cm
HABITAT: Tropical forests, particularly edges and clearings
RANGE: From India and Sri Lanka across south-east Asia to New Guinea
STATUS: Generally common

PEARL CRESCENT

PHYCIODES THAROS

The caterpillar of the Pearl Crescent feeds on asters: in meadows abundant with the flower, swarms of hundreds of these butterflies can be found. From above, the wings are orange with black borders and black markings, including veining, patches and spots. The underwings are a creamy yellow with brown veins. There are two distinct brown patches on the forewing and on the hindwing a pale crescent-shaped spot, hence its common name.

CATERPILLAR: Black body with fine white stripes on back and sides and dark spines. Feeds on aster
WINGSPAN: 3–3.5cm
HABITAT: Damp and dry meadows, prairies, woodland edges, roadsides and gardens
RANGE: Across North America from Canada to Mexico
STATUS: Common and widespread

COMMA
POLYGONIA C-ALBUM

CATERPILLAR: Black body with orange stripes, a white patch behind the neck and spines. Feeds on nettles and hops

WINGSPAN: 4–6cm

HABITAT: Flowery woodland, meadows, gardens, wasteland and roadsides

RANGE: Western and southern Europe, into Asia and north Africa

STATUS: Widespread and common

This butterfly has two main distinguishing features: its untidily scalloped wing-edges and brown underside enable it to closely resemble a dry leaf when at rest; and it bears a sharp white C mark, or comma, on its hindwing. From above the Comma has a background colour of rich orange which is marked with brown patches and spots and rufus edges with pale orange crescents. Its underwing colour is mottled brown, patterned to closely resemble a dead leaf. The white comma is in the centre of the hindwing. Its forewings are hooked at the top, with deep scallops running down both wing edges and short, rounded tails on the hindwing. It hibernates as a butterfly among dry leaves.

MOTHER-OF-PEARL BUTTERFLY
SALAMIS PARHASSUS

This large, beautiful butterfly has almost translucent wings; they are iridescent pale green shot with purple. In flight its scales catch the light, but at rest it becomes dull: effective camouflage amongst leaves. Its outer edges and hooked forewing tip are black and it has varying black spots on both wings. The hindwings are an irregular, jagged shape, with a short tail that is also black. Above the tail is a bright red, white and black eyespot which deters predators. Mother-of-Pearl Butterflies are unusual for their seasonal differences: during the wet season they are smaller.

CATERPILLAR: Black-brown body with bright red marks on back and spines. Feeds on acanthus

WINGSPAN: 7.5–10cm

HABITAT: Dense woodland, rainforests and forest riversides

RANGE: Across Africa south of the Sahara into South Africa

STATUS: Widespread and common

RED ADMIRAL

VANESSA ATALANTA

This is a well-known butterfly across the northern hemisphere, since it is a frequent garden visitor during the warm summer months. The Red Admiral migrates into the far north of its range in huge numbers; in Europe it is really only native to Mediterranean areas but under the right conditions will make its way to Iceland. Its upper side is a rich blackish brown with bold orange stripes across the forewing and along the hindwing margin. The tip of the forewing is marked with pure white spots. On the underside it is paler; the forewings are brown with patches of orange, white and black, whilst the hindwings have an intricate mottled brown pattern.

CATERPILLAR: Dark grey or green with hairs. Feeds on nettles
WINGSPAN: 5–6cm
HABITAT: A wide variety of habitats, wherever flowers and nettles can be found
RANGE: Across the northern hemisphere: from Canada to Central America; Europe into north Africa and India
STATUS: Widespread and common

INDIAN RED ADMIRAL

VANESSA INDICA

This species is very similar to its close relative the Red Admiral; however, it is slightly larger with broader wings and more squared inner hindwings. It is dark brown above with a broad orange band on the forewing which is marked with distinctive black spots. The black forewing tip has smaller white markings. The orange marginal band on the hindwing bears large black spots and there are small blue spots on the inner edge. From below it bears a close resemblance to the Red Admiral.

CATERPILLAR: Black and yellow body with dark spines. Feeds on nettle
WINGSPAN: 6–7cm
HABITAT: Flowery open land, grassland, meadows, roadsides, gardens
RANGE: From India and Pakistan into Japan and the Philippines
STATUS: Generally common

QUEEN OF SPAIN FRITILLARY
ARGYNNIS LATHONIA

CATERPILLAR: Black body with white spots, a pair of white lines along the back and brown spines. Feeds on violets

WINGSPAN: 4–5cm

HABITAT: Open lowlands, fields, meadows and flowery grassland

RANGE: From north Africa into Europe and Asia as far as India

STATUS: Widespread and common

The Queen of Spain Fritillary is a strong, fast-flying butterfly which migrates over long distances, reaching further north in its range during fine weather and even ascending to over 2,000 feet in search of feeding territories. From above it has orange wings patterned with black spots, with the outer wing margins highlighted by a double row of fine black lines. From below it has paler forewings with dark spots and creamy orange hindwings boldly marked with large silver patches.

SILVER WASHED FRITILLARY
ARGYNNIS PAPHIA

This relatively large fritillary can be identified partly by its size but also by its underside, which is a mixture of pale yellow-green and metallic, silvery white. From above it has typical fritillary markings, a bright orange background colour that is patterned with dark blackish brown spots and bars. The spots are organized in two stripes across the margins of both wings, the bars towards the centre of the forewing and along the leading edge. Females tend to lack these forewing bars. In both sexes the forewings are angular and long whereas the hindwings are large and rounded.

CATERPILLAR: Dark brown body with a pair of orange back stripes and brown spines. Feeds on violets
WINGSPAN: 6–7cm
HABITAT: Woodland, wooded clearings, hedgerows and parkland
RANGE: Across Europe towards north Africa and Asia
STATUS: Widespread and common

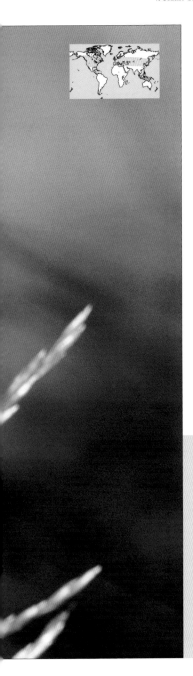

SMALL PEARL-BORDERED FRITILLARY
(SILVER-BORDERED FRITILLARY)

BOLORIA SELENE

This widespread fritillary is one of the most common types found in North America, where it is known as the Silver-bordered Fritillary. In Europe it is the Small Pearl-bordered Fritillary, and both common names refer to the intricate, metallic patterning on the underside of the hindwing. From above it is deep orange marked with black squares, spots and crescents. The underside forewing is a paler orange with scattered brown markings. The hindwing has a pattern of black veins, spots and orange and white patches. Distinguishing marks include seven white crescent spots on the hindwing margin and a small black eyespot in the centre of the hindwing.

CATERPILLAR: Brown body, white markings and pale brown spines. Feeds on violets
WINGSPAN: 3–4cm
HABITAT: A variety of habitats: woodland, clearings, open lowland and lower mountain slopes – wherever violets grow
RANGE: Across temperate North America, Europe and Asia
STATUS: Generally common

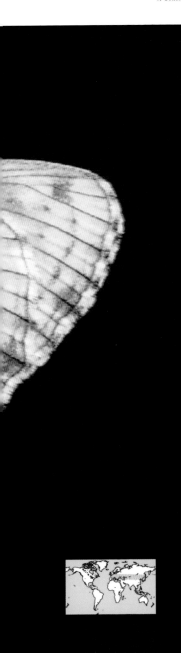

LESSER MARBLED FRITILLARY

BRENTHIS INO

This is a relatively small but otherwise typical fritillary butterfly. It has upper-side wings that are orange marked with a chequered pattern of black spots. The wing-edges are scalloped and bordered with black. Its body and wing bases are also dark. On its underside the wings are more yellow, with black and white edges to both wings. The forewings bear black spots, the hindwings a combination of yellow, brown and buff patches.

CATERPILLAR: Black body with a pair of white stripes and brown back spines. Feeds on raspberry leaves, great burnet and meadowsweet
WINGSPAN: 3–4cm
HABITAT: Flowery, damp grassland and meadows, marshland
RANGE: Central and northern Europe, excluding the British Isles, into Asia and Japan
STATUS: Locally common

MARSH FRITILLARY EURODRYAS AURINIA

CATERPILLAR: Black body
with white spots and
spines. Feeds on
scabious and plantain
WINGSPAN: 4–5cm
HABITAT: Open grassland,
marshes, dry moorland
RANGE: Across western
Europe towards central
Asia
STATUS: Widespread with
fluctuating numbers,
though generally
common

This common fritillary has relatively narrow wings
which can aid identification. From above its colouring is
an even mixture of orange, cream and brown in a
delicate mosaic patterning. The design of this pattern is
not regular but can vary between butterflies from
different areas. The wings are edged with a fine white
fringe and the dark brown wing border bears small
white crescents. It also has small black spots within the
orange band that lines the outer margin of the hindwing.
Its underside is similarly patterned but with a paler
colouring and less black.

MELITAEA DIDYMA SPOTTED FRITILLARY

This variable species is always consistent in its wing shape, having broad, rounded wings. Its upper-side background colour is usually bright orange, although this can vary from region to region and females are generally paler, particularly on the forewing. Some females are almost grey in colour, which can make identification difficult. There is a pattern of black spots and black wing borders and a fine white fringe marked with black. The underside is more regular, with alternating bands of orange and cream marked with black spots.

CATERPILLAR: White with black lines and red back spots plus spines. Feeds on plantains

WINGSPAN: 3–5cm

HABITAT: Open, flowery grassland, scrubland, meadows and roadsides

RANGE: Southern Europe, north Africa and cooler Asia

STATUS: Generally common

GREAT SPANGLED FRITILLARY

SPEYERIA CYBELE

This large fritillary is a common sight across North America, where it can be identified by its combination of dark colouring at the wing bases and bright orange at the outer edges. The broad wings have scalloped edges and these are accentuated by the dark crescent spots on the margins. The forewing also shows a band of dark spots along the edge; smaller spots appear on the hindwing. The orange background colour can be paler in some regions. From below the wings show more orange than brown and the hindwing has a number of distinctive silvery spots at the centre and the outer edge.

CATERPILLAR: Black with orange spines. Feeds on violets
WINGSPAN: 5.5–7.5cm
HABITAT: Woodland clearings, meadows, pasture and gardens
RANGE: Across North America from Canada towards New Mexico
STATUS: Common and widespread

REGAL FRITILLARY SPEYERIA IDALIA

CATERPILLAR: Black and yellow body with short, branching spines. Feeds on bird's-foot and prairie violets
WINGSPAN: 7–9cm
HABITAT: Tall-grass prairies
RANGE: Limited to some states of North America including Pennsylvania and Illinois
STATUS: Declining

The Regal Fritillary is a sad example of the detrimental effect of habitat loss on butterfly populations. This attractive fritillary is in sharp decline, having disappeared from many of its former ranges across the tall-grass prairies of central North America. It is large, with broad, squared wings. From above the forewings are a bright orange colour with black markings and a broad black border spotted with white. The hindwings are black with two rows of marginal white spots. From below the repeated spotting appears more metallic and the background colour of the wings is similarly dark.

AGLAIS URICAE SMALL TORTOISESHELL

One of Europe's most common and well known butterflies, the Small Tortoiseshell has bright, colourful upperwings that make it easy to recognize. From above the background colour is orange-red, marked with square patches of dark brown or black and creamy yellow. These patches form a broad band along the leading edge of the forewing. Along the raggedly scalloped edges of both wings is a broad black border chequered with pale blue spots. On its underside the Small Tortoiseshell is far duller in appearance, with blackish-brown wings with a pale brown border. The forewing bears a pale patch. Late-summer and autumn broods will hibernate as butterflies, usually in barns, lofts and stables.

CATERPILLAR: Yellow-and black-striped body covered in yellow spines. Groups of caterpillars feed on nettle leaves

WINGSPAN: 5cm

HABITAT: Open flowery areas: meadows, fields, roadsides, gardens, lower mountain slopes

RANGE: Across Europe into Asia and Japan

STATUS: Common and widespread

CAMBERWELL BEAUTY/ MOURNING CLOAK

NYMPHALIS ANTIOPA

Commonly known as the Camberwell Beauty in Europe and the Mourning Cloak in America, this butterfly is widespread but not necessarily easy to observe. As woodland butterflies that feed on tree sap, they only occasionally come down to the ground to feed off flowers. Both males and females are a deep maroon colour bordered with light yellow and a band of bright blue spots on the outer edges. From below they are dark grey with black lines and white wing margins speckled with black. The butterfly hibernates in tree hollows over winter, but will often emerge on warm early-spring days.

CATERPILLAR: Black body with white spots and red back markings. Feeds on deciduous trees
WINGSPAN: 6–8cm
HABITAT: Deciduous woodland, gardens and parkland; any open lowland with appropriate trees
RANGE: North America, Europe and cooler regions of Asia
STATUS: Widespread but not common; declining in some areas

LARGE TORTOISESHELL
NYMPHALIS POLYCHLOROS

CATERPILLAR: Black body with white spots and orange spines. Feeds on tree foliage

WINGSPAN: 5–6cm

HABITAT: Deciduous woodland, hedgerows, gardens; wherever elms and willows can be found

RANGE: From western Europe across to Asia

STATUS: Widespread and generally common, although numbers have suffered through damage to habitat, particularly from diseased elms

The Large Tortoiseshell is bigger and hairier than its small namesake, and is slightly less bright and distinctive. The background colour of the upperwings is orange; there are black patches and spots on the forewing and a single patch on the hindwing. The leading edge of the forewing is marked with both black and yellow patches. The ragged wing-edges bear a broad black band marked with yellow, and on the hindwing edge small blue crescents can be observed. The underside is mottled brown with a blue-grey marginal band. The Large Tortoiseshell hibernates as a butterfly, chosing tree hollows, its preferred habitat, and sometimes caves, barns and sheds. It feeds on tree sap.

GULF FRITILLARY
AGRAULIS VANILLAE

A common butterfly across the southern states of North America, the Gulf Fritillary is a regular visitor to well stocked parks and gardens. From above its wings have a background colour of bright reddish orange, marked with dark brown streaks and spots. There are three distinguishing black and white eyespots near the leading edge of the forewing; the hindwing has a distinctive dark-ringed border. From below the wings have a more brownish-orange background colour, and both bear large, elongated and irregularly shaped silver patches with dark edges. Males and females are similar.

CATERPILLAR: Orange body with rows of black, branching spines. Feeds on passionflowers

WINGSPAN: 6.5–7.5cm

HABITAT: Parks and gardens, woodland edges, open scrubland

RANGE: Central America and the West Indies up to southern states of North America

STATUS: Common and widespread

JULIA/FLAMBEAU DRYAS IULIA

CATERPILLAR: Brown spiny body. Feeds on passionflower
WINGSPAN: 7–9cm
HABITAT: Subtropical woodland edges, open edges, Florida Everglades
RANGE: From South and Central America up to southern states of the USA
STATUS: Generally common

In some areas the Julia is known as the Flambeau and its long, narrow wings are indeed a flaming orange-red colour from above. The bright upperwing is delicately marked with black veins, and whilst males have a dark forewing spot on the leading edge, females have a black band that crosses the forewing. Both sexes are finely edged with black and the scalloped hindwing also bears orange crescent spots. From underneath the Julia is a paler orange-brown with creamy white markings on the hindwing fringe. Typically, this brightly coloured butterfly is also poisonous.

HELICONIUS CHARITHONIA ZEBRA

Like many other Heliconius butterflies, the Zebra collects and feeds on the pollen and nectar of forest flowers. It has black wings which are boldly marked with yellow bands, three on the forewing and one solid band across the centre of the hindwing, plus a broken band along the hindwing margin. Its underside is similar but with the addition of red spots at the wing bases. In order to ensure a virgin mate, males prefer to mate with females as they are drying after emerging from their pupa.

CATERPILLAR: White body with black spines and spots. Feeds on passionflower

WINGSPAN: 7–8cm

HABITAT: Dense tropical woodland edges and clearings

RANGE: Southern states of the USA to Central and South America and the West Indies

STATUS: Generally common, although threatened by loss of habitat

HELICONIUS MIMIC

EUEIDES ISABELLA

An attractive mimic butterfly, the Heliconius Mimic or Isabella's Heliconian has broad, narrow, rounded forewings and smaller, rounded hindwings. Its coloration is similar to that of a number of other Heliconius species, poisonous models for a number of mimics. The Isabella has similar markings on both sides of its wings, although it is duller below. The forewings have a background colour of brown with orange stripes on the inner, basal edge and yellow patches towards the outer tips. The underwings are broadly striped with orange and brown and the brown marginal edge is marked with small white spots.

CATERPILLAR: Black body with white bands across the back. Feeds on passionflower
WINGSPAN: 5–7cm
HABITAT: Sub-tropical forests, clearings and edges
RANGE: South and Central America, into southern states of the USA
STATUS: Generally common

THE POSTMAN

HELICONIUS MELPOMENE

This slow-flying butterfly avoids bright sunlight, keeping to the shadier parts of the forest edges which it inhabits. Like other Heliconia it has long, narrow wings, but its coloration is very variable since different subspecies will mimic the subspecies of *Heliconius erato* – the Small Postman. In general it will have a background colour of black with a variety of red and yellow markings on both wings. From below, the markings are repeated, but the colours are more muted.

CATERPILLAR: White body with black spots, orange head and spines. Feeds on passionflower
WINGSPAN: 6–8cm
HABITAT: Subtropical forest edges
RANGE: Central and South America and the West Indies
STATUS: Generally common

SWEET OIL MECHANITIS POLYMNIA

CATERPILLAR: Pale green back and yellow sides with yellow side spines. Feeds on solanum leaves, particularly deadly nightshade
WINGSPAN: 6–7.5cm
HABITAT: A variety of habitats, including forest edges, fields, roadsides and urban areas
RANGE: From Mexico into South America
STATUS: Generally common

This is a particularly common butterfly in South America and is regularly seen flying through built-up areas and city streets. Its ability to adapt to disrupted habitats has earned it the alternative common name Disturbed Tigerwing. A poisonous species, it is the model for a large number of mimics. It has a long, narrow forewing which is orange at the base then yellow leading to a black tip. The coloured wing is marked with black patches. The hindwings are orange with a broad central black band and a black margin. On the underside both wing margins are spotted with blue.

DANAUS CHRYSIPPUS PLAIN TIGER

This butterfly is also known as the African Monarch, due to its familial resemblance to its close relative *Danaus plexippus*. It is a strong flier, with a slow, bouncing flight style, and migrates long distances. It has broad, pointed forewings which are orange in colour with black tips bearing white spots. The hindwings are creamy white with orange and black edges and a series of dark spots in the centre of the wing; the number of these varies between different individuals. The underside is similar but paler. As a successful poisonous butterfly, the Plain Tiger is the model for a number of mimics.

CATERPILLAR: Orange-, black- and white-banded body. Feeds on milkweed

WINGSPAN: 7–8cm

HABITAT: A variety: open fields, gardens, forests edges

RANGE: Across Africa, Asia, Australia, Japan and Malaysia

STATUS: Widespread and common

QUEEN

DANAUS GILIPPUS

In appearance the Queen butterfly is similar to its close relative the Monarch; however it is smaller in size and slightly darker in appearance, with far less patterning on the upper side. From above the background colour of the wings is a deep orange-brown with darker brown wing margins. There are white spots on the tip of the forewing and scattered along the margins. Males also show scent scales on the centre hindwing as a small pale-grey mark. The underside is a slightly paler orange-brown with distinctive black veins edged with white. The white spots on the black wing margins are bold, as are the white spots marking the black body and abdomen.

CATERPILLAR: Grey body with black rings spotted with orange. Feeds on milkweed
WINGSPAN: 7–7.5cm
HABITAT: Open areas, grassland, scrub, deserts and prairies
RANGE: Southern states of the USA into Central and South America
STATUS: Common

QUEEN

DANAUS GILIPPUS

In appearance the Queen butterfly is similar to its close relative the Monarch; however it is smaller in size and slightly darker in appearance, with far less patterning on the upper side. From above the background colour of the wings is a deep orange-brown with darker brown wing margins. There are white spots on the tip of the forewing and scattered along the margins. Males also show scent scales on the centre hindwing as a small pale-grey mark. The underside is a slightly paler orange-brown with distinctive black veins edged with white. The white spots on the black wing margins are bold, as are the white spots marking the black body and abdomen.

CATERPILLAR: Grey body with black rings spotted with orange. Feeds on milkweed
WINGSPAN: 7–7.5cm
HABITAT: Open areas, grassland, scrub, deserts and prairies
RANGE: Southern states of the USA into Central and South America
STATUS: Common

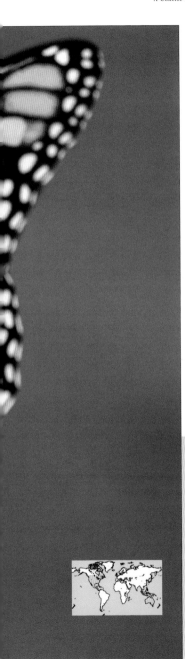

MONARCH

DANAUS PLEXIPPUS

This well known migrant is a striking orange colour with distinctive black veining, a warning to predators that it is poisonous. Both wings bear black marginal bands marked with bright white spots, a pattern that is repeated on its body and abdomen. The pointed forewings have a black tip which has three distinctive orange patches. The underside is similar but paler, and males have a small black scent patch on their hindwings. A very strong flier, swarms of Monarchs travel in huge numbers heading south from Canada to Mexico during autumn. When the wind blows in the right direction many are swept off course towards Europe and Australasia.

CATERPILLAR: Black, yellow and cream bands with black tentacles behind the head. Feeds on milkweed
WINGSPAN: 7–10cm
HABITAT: Open land, fields, roadsides, prairies and gardens
RANGE: Native to the Americas, vagrant to Australasia, the Canary Islands and Europe
STATUS: Common in the Americas, scarcer in migrant countries

HESPERIIDAE
SKIPPERS

CHEQUERED SKIPPER
CARTEROCEPHALUS PALAEMON

CATERPILLAR: Pale creamy brown with pink stripes. Feeds on grasses

WINGSPAN: 2–3cm

HABITAT: Grassland, woodland edges and clearings

RANGE: Cold and temperate North America, Europe and Asia

STATUS: Widespread and common

The distinctive patterning on this widespread skipper makes it relatively easy to identify, particularly since it likes to rest with its wings open. It has upperwings that are predominantly dark brown with orange markings arranged in a chequerboard pattern. On the underside the colour is much paler with the marking repeated in a buff colour. Males are highly territorial and can be observed keeping watch over their area from tree branches or tall grasses. It has a preference for colder climates, hence its American common name, the Arctic Skipper. Like many skippers, the adult Chequered Skipper lay eggs singly on the leaves of grasses. The young caterpillar creates a tent by pulling the edges of the leaves together and binding them with silk threads.

SILVER-SPOTTED SKIPPER
EPARGYREUS CLARUS

Skippers are called so because of their habit of flying from plant to plant in short 'skips'. There are over 3,000 different species. The Silver-spotted Skipper is one of the most conspicuous, being is a relatively large skipper, with elongated hindwings and small, blunt tails. On its upper-side the Silver-spotted Skipper has a background colour of dark brown with orange patches on the forewing. This patch is repeated on the underside of the butterfly, but the colouring is much paler and more translucent. The butterfly earns it common name from the distinctive silver patch that marks the centre of the underside hindwing. It has a distinctively wide head, and antennae with a curved tip.

CATERPILLAR: Light green with darker patches and a red head
WINGSPAN: 4–6cm
HABITAT: Woodland edges, brush and fields
RANGE: Found across North America
STATUS: Widespread and common

LARGE SKIPPER

OCHLODES VENATAS

The Large Skipper has a background colour of olive-brown on its wings, which in males is suffused with orange, making them much brighter. Males can also be distinguished by their sex brand, the black line on the forewing which is formed from scent scales. Its wings are a rich ruddy brown above and much paler yellow-brown below, and on the upper side the veins are displayed in a darker blackish brown. Females tend to be duller, with a darker background brown which bears dull yellow spots on both upper-side wings. When at rest it holds its wings open at a slight angle, enabling identification with a view of both sides

CATERPILLAR: Green body. Feeds on grasses
WINGSPAN: 3cm
HABITAT: Open grassland, woodland edges and clearings, flowery meadows and hedgerows
RANGE: Across Europe into Asia as far as Japan
STATUS: Generally common

DINGY SKIPPER ERYNNIS TAGES

CATERPILLAR: Pale green with a black line along back ,and black head. Feeds on members of the pea family, particularly crown vetch
WINGSPAN: 2.5cm
HABITAT: Flowery grassland, meadows and lower mountain slopes
RANGE: Western and northern Europe into northern Asia and China
STATUS: Common, though numbers are in decline

Often found in meadows and grassland, this small brown butterfly could easily be mistaken for a moth (such as the Mother Shipton moth) with its stout abdomen and buzzing flight. It also resembles the Grizzled Skipper which can be similar in colour. Its dark mottled upperwings provide excellent camouflage; the forewings are patterned with dark brown on a greyish-brown background, while the hindwings are brown with small white spots along the marginal edge. From below, the Dingy Skipper is a paler brown with the white marginal spots repeated. It has a preference for cooler climates.

PYRGUS MALVAE GRIZZLED SKIPPER

The Grizzled Skipper is a widespread but unfortunately declining example of the genus *Pyrgus*, skippers with white spot markings. It has the characteristic skipper shape, with the length of the body and wings being roughly equal (in other butterflies the wings tend to be longer). On its upper side the background colour is brown and this bears small, squarish, white spots in a chequered pattern. The wing-edges are uniformly chequered in brown and white. It is paler on the underside and the white markings are larger, particularly on the hindwing, which bears a large central white patch. Its body is darker above and paler below, mirroring the colours of the wings.

CATERPILLAR: Green with a large black head. Feeds on potentilla and wild strawberry
WINGSPAN: 2–2.5cm
HABITAT: Woodland edges and clearings, heaths, grassy meadows
RANGE: Across Europe into Asia towards Mongolia
STATUS: Locally common, but in decline

LULWORTH SKIPPER

THYMELICUS ACTION

This is a fast-flying and active little butterfly which can be found on a range of grasslands. The background colour of its wings is an olive brown, and on females the forewing shows delicate patches of yellow on the upper side. Males are marked with a fine black line across the forewing and their wing colour is more yellowy than the females'. When basking, the Lulworth Skipper raises its forewings slightly, while keeping the hindwings in a horizontal position. This typical skipper attitude is thought to aid the absorption of the sun's energy.

CATERPILLAR: Pale green, with darker green back. Feeds on grasses
WINGSPAN: 2.5cm
HABITAT: Open grassland and meadows
RANGE: Western and southern Europe into Asia
STATUS: Generally common

ESSEX SKIPPER THYMELICUS LINEOLA

CATERPILLAR: Pale green with yellow stripes. Feeds on grasses
WINGSPAN: 2.5cm
HABITAT: Flowery fields, meadows, roadside verges
RANGE: North Africa, Europe and Asia, North America
STATUS: Generally common

Almost identical to its close relative the Small Skipper (*Thymelicus sylvestris*), the Essex Skipper can be distinguished only by the darker colour of its antennae. Unlike many other skippers, it overwinters as an egg rather than a caterpillar. Its wings are an attractive rusty orange colour on both sides, the only significant markings are the slightly darker wing-edges and the paler fringe. It is fairly widespread: in areas inhabited by Essex Skippers, they can appear in large numbers. In the United States and Canada, this introduced butterfly is commonly known as the European Skipper.

URBANUS PROTEUS LONG-TAILED SKIPPER

In most respects this is a typical skipper butterfly. However, it has two remarkable distinguishing features: proportionally long tail streamers and an iridescent-green colouring on the upper side of the wings. From above, the wings are rich brown in colour with a series of white patches on the tips of the forewings. The hindwings and tails are a similar brown without any markings. The green scaling extends from the body and base of the wings and reaches on to the tails. From below, both wings show brown, black and white patterning, while the tails are solid brown. In the southern states of the United States this attractive butterfly can become a pest in bean crops, where it is known as the 'bean leaf roller'.

CATERPILLAR: Olive body with brown stripes, yellow and black spots. Feeds on phaseolus

WINGSPAN: 4–5.5cm

HABITAT: Open fields, scrubland, wasteland and agricultural land

RANGE: From South America up towards southern states of the USA

STATUS: Generally common

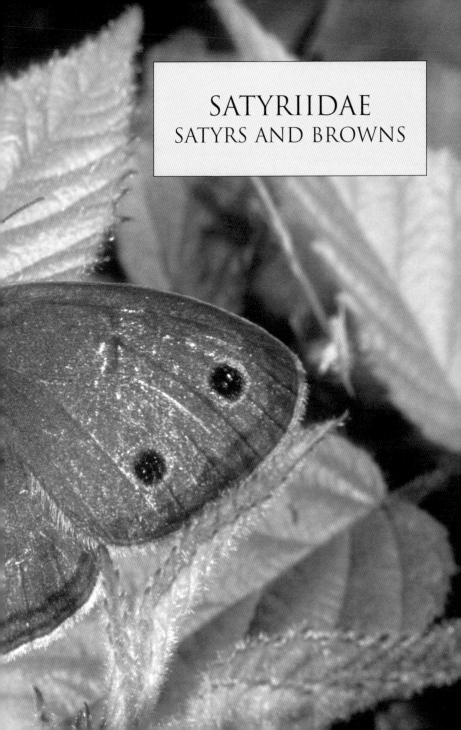

SATYRIIDAE
SATYRS AND BROWNS

RINGLET APHANTOPUS HYPERANTUS

CATERPILLAR: Pale olive green, with fine yellow and black stripes. Feeds on grasses

WINGSPAN: 4–5cm

HABITAT: Low-level open grassland, meadows, roadside verges, hedgerows and woodland edges

RANGE: Across Europe into Asia

STATUS: Widespread and common

The Ringlet is a common European and Asian butterfly, and a typical example of a Satyr; it is small and brown and bears a prominent band of small eyespots. On its upper side the Ringlet is dark brown; in males this can be almost black. Each wing bears a pair of small dark eyespots, which are not always apparent. The underside is a much paler brown and the eyespots are highly visible, black ringed with yellow with a white highlight. There are often five eyespots on the hindwing and three on the fore; however the number and size of these distinctive markings does vary. It is thought that these eyespots confuse predators as to the position of the butterfly's body.

COENONYMPHA ARCANIA PEARLY HEATH

This small, European grassland butterfly rarely reveals its upperwings when resting, but when flying it is possible to see a flash of its orange wings. Its upper side is mainly brown, with orange forewings edged with dark brown. On the underside, the orange-brown forewing bears a small black eyespot with white highlight. The hindwing is grey-brown with a buff-coloured steak and an orange marginal band. There are several eyespots lined along the marginal edge; these are black ringed with orange with a white highlight. An additional eyespot can be observed on the inner edge of the hindwing.

CATERPILLAR: Green with white side stripe. Feeds on grasses

WINGSPAN: 3.5cm

HABITAT: Grassy slopes, mountain foothills and open woodland

RANGE: Across western Europe into western Asia

STATUS: Generally common

SMALL HEATH COENONYMPHA PAMPHILUS

CATERPILLAR: Pale green
body with yellow
stripes. Feeds on grasses
WINGSAPN: 3cm
HABITAT: Open grassland,
meadows, heath and
roadside verges
RANGE: Across northern
Europe, including Britain
and Scandinavia
STATUS: Locally common,
threatened by loss of
habitat

On its upper side the Small Heath has solid orange-
brown forewings, and similarly coloured hindwings
with a pale patch at the inner edge and grey borders.
From below it is more grey, with grey hindwings that
are distinguished by a pale wavy band across the centre
of the wing. The forewing is orange-brown with grey
margins and a pale-ringed black eyespot with white
highlight. Since the Small Heath tends to rest with its
wings closed, its underside is that which is most often
observed. The male and female look very similar, the
main distinction being that the female is slightly larger.

COENONYMPHA TULLIA LARGE HEATH

In Europe this butterfly is commonly known as the Large Heath, in North America as the Ringlet, and in appearance it is not too dissimilar from the European Ringlet. This neat little grassland butterfly has a variable background colouring, from creamy yellow to brown; however, its distinguishing feature is the eyespots, which are more bold on the underside of the wings. There is always a small round black eyespot on the tip of the forewing; this is both ringed and highlighted with white on the underside. On the hindwing there is a row of similar eyespots, the number of which can vary. The Large Heath has a characteristic flight pattern, keeping close the ground on windy days.

CATERPILLAR: Green body, dark green back and white side stripes. Feeds on sedge and cottongrass

WINGSPAN: 4cm

HABITAT: Grasses, hillsides, meadows and lower mountain slopes

RANGE: Central and northern Europe into Asia, across the United States into Canada

STATUS: Widespread and common

LITTLE WOOD SATYR

EUPTYCHIA CYMELA

The eyespots on this Satyr are its most distinguishing feature. It has rich-brown wings edged with a pair of fine dark lines. The pair of eyespots on each wing are black and ringed with orange, and each bears a pair of silvery-blue highlights. On its underside the Little Wood Satyr is a paler brown colour and the prominent eyespots are repeated. The outer wing margins are marked with a series of fine stripes and the eyespots are connected by a series of small metallic spots. These butterflies can occasionally be observed feeding from bird droppings.

CATERPILLAR: Brown body with tiny white spots. Feeds on grasses
WINGSPAN: 4.5–5cm
HABITAT: Brushland, wooded clearings and woodland edges
RANGE: Across eastern half of North America, from Canada to Mexico
STATUS: Generally common

GRAYLING HIPPARCHIA SEMELE

CATERPILLAR: Brown body with black stripes. Feeds on grasses
WINGSPAN: 5cm
HABITAT: Dry rocky grassland and cliffs, meadows and lower mountain slopes
RANGE: Across Europe into Asia
STATUS: Generally common

This small butterfly is an expert at camouflage; it likes to bask on tree trunks and bare rock, and not only is its wing pattern designed to merge in with such a background, it also holds its wings at a slight angle to avoid casting any shadow. On its upper side it has pale, dull-brown wings with buff and orange patches and brown eyespots. The underwings, which are more likely to be observed, are mottled grey and brown on the hindwing. The brighter forewing is often tucked behind the resting hindwing, whereby its buff and orange patch and two black eyespots are less noticeable to predators.

MANIOLA TITHONIUS GATEKEEPER

This particularly common member of the brown family is in abundance during midsummer, particularly when brambles are in flower. It is a small butterfly, with bright orange upperwings that are broadly bordered with brown across both wing margins. The forewing also bears a brown central patch and a black eyespot marked with a pair of white highlights. Males also bear a dark sex patch on the forewing. On the underside both wings are much paler, a buff yellow on the forewing and marbled lighter browns on the hindwing. The forewing eyespot is repeated below.

CATERPILLAR: Green body with darker green side stripes. Feeds on grasses

WINGSPAN: 4cm

HABITAT: Open grassy land, meadows, hedgerows and woodland edges

RANGE: Across western and southern Europe towards Turkey

STATUS: Generally common

MEADOW BROWN

MANIOLA JURTINA

This common grassland butterfly is a strong, fast flier and the males are highly territorial, patrolling their area keeping watch for other males. Identification is easier when the underside is observed, since the upper side of the Meadow Brown is particularly variable, both between the sexes and across the range. In general from above it is a rich brown colour with an orange patch near the tip of the forewing which bears the large dark eyespot. Females are more sharply coloured, often showing far more orange than the males, many of which can show no orange at all. From below the wings are much paler: the forewing is orange and buff brown with the dark eyespot, the hindwing brown with a broad buff band which bears small dark spots.

CATERPILLAR: Green body with yellow side stripe and yellow hairs. Feeds on grasses
WINGSPAN: 5–5.5cm
HABITAT: Grassland, meadows, roadsides, woodland edges and clearings
RANGE: Across Europe into central Asia
STATUS: Widespread and common

MARBLED WHITE

MELANGARIA GALATHEA

This is an attractive black-and-white-patterned butterfly with a very apt common name. On the upper side of its wings it is distinctively grounded with dark blackish brown which bears a marbled pattern of white patches. There is a large basal patch on both wings and also white crescents on the brown margins. On the underside, more white shows, with black veins and grey patches as well as a black line edging the outer wing margins. There is also a grey band marked with eyespots on the hindwing. Males and females are similar, although females have a yellowish hindwing on the underside.

CATERPILLAR: Pale green with dark line along the back. Feeds on grasses
WINGSPAN: 5cm
HABITAT: Low-lying, flowery grassland, meadows and roadside verges
RANGE: Western and central Europe into north Africa and Asia
STATUS: Widespread and commonly found in colonies

DRYAD BUTTERFLY MINIOS DRYAS

CATERPILLAR: Creamy white speckled with dark and two brown stripes extending from the forked tail. Feeds on grasses
WINGSPAN: 5–7cm
HABITAT: Dry, open grassland, low slopes and open woodland
RANGE: Southern Europe into Asia and Japan
STATUS: Locally common

Male and female Dryad Butterflies are dimorphic, or dissimilar; however both are relatively easy to identify, for different reasons. The male is smaller and has upperwings which are almost solid black; the forewing, however, bears a pair of blue eyespots that are almost impossible to see. From underneath it is mottled grey and brown and the forewing bears a single dark eyespot. The female is much paler, with upperwings that are rich brown, and the two blue eyespots are a prominent feature, as is the single blue eyespot on the hindwing. The underside is similar to that of the male. Both sexes have scalloped hindwings; this feature is much more pronounced in the female.

PARARGE AEGERIA SPECKLED WOOD

The speckled brown patterning on this woodland butterfly gives it effective camouflage in the dappled light of its woodland habitat. On its upper side it has a background colour of rich brown which is marked on the forewings with creamy yellow patches and on the hindwing with a row of bold eyespots – black ringed with cream and highlighted with white. The markings on the hindwings can appear orange in some areas, particularly in the south of its range. On its underside the hindwing eyespots are less clear to see, lacking the black; however the forewing bears a more prominent black spot at the tip. The underside has a more marbled brown appearance. Like several other butterflies (notably the skippers) the Speckled Brown shows a high degree of territorial behaviour.

CATERPILLAR: Pale green with dark green back and fine side stripes. Feeds on couch grass
WINGSPAN: 4.5cm
HABITAT: Mature, deciduous woodland
RANGE: Across Europe into Asia
STATUS: Common in its habitat

WALL BROWN

PARARGE MEGERA

This striking orange Satyr can often be observed sunbathing with its wings spread open. It has upperwings grounded in rich orange and patterned with dark veins, bands and patches. Its gently scalloped and rounded wings are edged with dark brown and the pale fringe is chequered with brown. There is a row of black eyespots hightlighted with white on the hindwing and one prominent and similar eyespot on the forewing. On its underside the patterning is repeated on to a paler background of buff, grey and brown. The hindwing is almost marbled in these colours, a design that provides effective camouflage.

CATERPILLAR: Green with a white side stripe. Feeds on grasses
WINGSPAN: 4.5cm
HABITAT: Dry heaths, hillsides and cliffs
RANGE: Across Europe into Asia
STATUS: Although widespread, the Wall Brown is in general decline

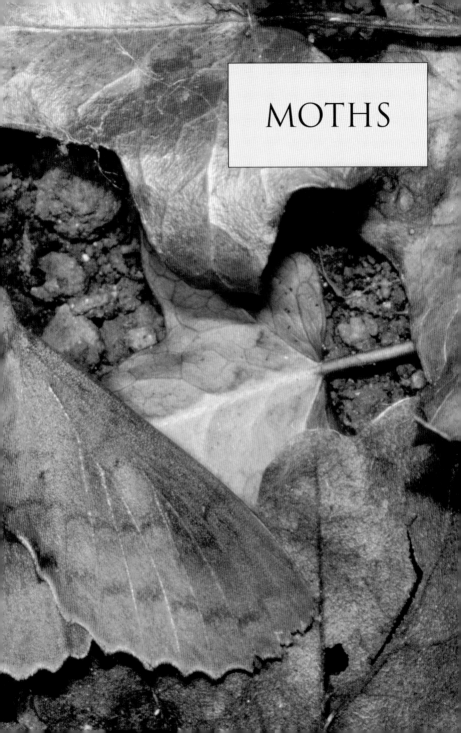

MOTHS

GARDEN TIGER MOTH

ARCTIA CAJA

This beautiful moth has strikingly different markings on its forewings and hindwings. The forewings have a creamy white background which is marked with either dark brown or black patches, a design that provides effective camouflage in the still moth. The hindwings are a contrasting flame-orange colour with black-ringed grey spots. The body is also orange, marked with black bands. A startled Garden Tiger will flash its bright hindwings which alarms any potential predator. Like most Arctid moths, its caterpillar is covered in poisonous spines and is commonly referred to as a 'woolly bear'.

CATERPILLAR: Black body covered in long black hairs with red hairs at the base. Feeds on a variety of low shrubs
WINGSPAN: 5–7cm
HABITAT: Parks and gardens and other cultivated land, roadsides, wasteland
RANGE: Mainly Europe into cooler Asia across to Japan. Also found in North America
STATUS: Widespread but declining, particularly in North America

GIANT LEOPARD MOTH
HYPERCOMPE SCRIBONIA

CATERPILLAR: Black hairy body, with usually invisible scarlet rings along segments
WINGSPAN: 6–9cm
HABITAT: Agricultural land, orchards, woodland edges, parks and gardens
RANGE: From south-eastern Canada down through eastern United states towards Mexico
STATUS: Generally common

A relatively large Arctid moth, the Giant Leopard Moth has strikingly patterned forewings which aid identification. The background colour is pure white covered with dark brown, ring-like markings and solid spots; this is continued on the moth's thorax and the back of its head. The hindwings lack these ring markings, instead they are solid white with dark brown spots along the outer edges. Males and females are similar, although the male has a dark yellowish-brown margin along the inner edge of the hindwing which the larger female lacks. The moth's abdomen is blue-black marked with dark yellow spots and its black legs have distinctive white bands.

WHITE ERMINE
SPILOSOMA LUBRICIPEDA

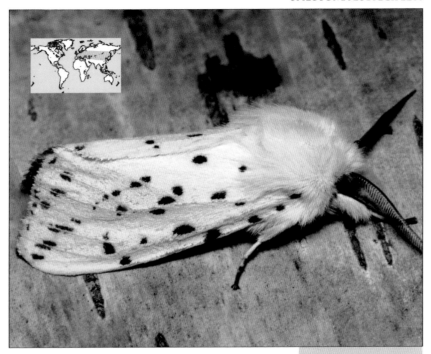

This relatively small Arctid moth has forewings that closely resemble the fur of its mammalian namesake, being pure white with black dots. Its hindwings are predominantly white; the only significant marking is a black spot on the inner edge of the wing. Its abdomen is a bright orange colour with lines of black spots, a warning to potential predators of its inedible status. The head and thorax are covered in white fur. In some areas colour variations can be found: the white can be more creamy yellow, or alternatively more or fewer black spots can be seen.

CATERPILLAR: Black hairy body with red-coloured line along back. Fast moving and feeds on most plants

WINGSPAN: 3–5cm

HABITAT: Found in a wide variety of habitats

RANGE: Across Europe and Asia towards Japan

STATUS: Widespread and common

SILKMOTH

BOMBYX MORI

Possibly the most famous moth of all, the Silkmoth is a member of the Bombycid family, most of which are native to east Asia and all of which spin strong silken cocoons. The *Bombyx mori* is the moth most usually associated with the production of silk for human use, and it has been bred in captivity for over 4,000 years so that it now no longer exists in the wild. Its wings are a creamy white or pale brown colour with visible veins and a slight hook at the forewing tip. Its stocky, furred body matches the wing colouring and the head lacks mouthparts, leaving it unable to feed as an adult. It is the caterpillars that provide the silk, and these are commercially raised in huge numbers; they do not survive the silk-extraction process.

CATERPILLAR: Pale, white body with pinkish eyespots along the back. Fed on Mulberry leaves
WINGSPAN: 4–6cm
HABITAT: Bred in captivity
RANGE: Originated in China
STATUS: Wild colonies are extinct; huge numbers in captivity worldwide

OWL MOTH

BRAHMAEA WALLICHII

This large moth is a striking example of the small Brahmaeid family – large, brown, highly patterned moths. The Owl Moth earns its name from the large owl's-eye-like eyespots at the base of the forewing. Both wings have a background colour of rich brown which is intricately patterned with regular bars and waves of darker brown. The solid-brown forewing tips bear rows of white crescents and both wings are bordered with pale brown then decorated with brown and white crescents. The eyespots bear three or more small dark dots. Its stocky body is dark brown banded and striped with pale brown.

CATERPILLAR: White and yellow body with black spots. Feeds on ash, privet and liliac.
WINGSPAN: 10–16cm
HABITAT: Open woodland, both deciduous and sub tropical
RANGE: East Asia, from India to China and Japan
STATUS: Generally locally common

LARGE EMERALD GEOMETRA PAPILIONARIA

CATERPILLAR: Pale green
looper. Feeds on birch
and alder trees
WINGSPAN: 5–6.5cm
HABITAT: Open woodland
and forest edges,
heathland.
RANGE: Across Europe, into
Asia towards Japan
STATUS: Widespread and
common

This large, robust Geometrid moth has, as its name
suggests, bright green wing colouring. Freshly emerged
examples are the most vivid, the solid green contrasting
clearly with a a pair of delicate white scalloped lines
which run across both wings. Older examples and
displayed specimens tend to be faded, becoming a paler
grey-green colour. The wings are broad and the
hindwings in particular are gently scalloped at the
rounded outer edges. Although males and females are
similar, males can be identified by their more feathered
antennae.

LYCIA HIRTARIA BRINDLED BEAUTY

The Brindled Beauty is a brown and white European example of a Geometrid moth. It is particularly effective at camouflage and as a consequence its colouring will vary depending upon its chosen habitat; species in more industrialized areas will often be darker. It rests upon tree trunks, and therefore both wings are a mottled brown and white to resemble bark. Its stocky body is furred, as are its wings – both sexes are able to fly. The male has broadly feathered antennae and tends to be a darker colour. Typically, its caterpillar is a looper.

CATERPILLAR: Dark brown or olive green with pale spots. Feeds on tree foliage

WINGSPAN: 4–5cm

HABITAT: Open woodland, orchards, parks and gardens

RANGE: Across western and northern Europe

STATUS: Very common; caterpillar can be considered a pest

SWALLOWTAILED MOTH

OURAPTERYX SAMUBUCARIA

A relatively large Geometrid, the Swallow-tailed moth has a particularly striking appearance and if discovered by day is often mistaken for a butterfly. It is however, a nocturnal moth and is more usually observed resting on lighted windows. Its wings are broad and the forewings are pointed whilst the hindwings bear short pointed, tails similar to those found on Swallowtail butterflies. Both wings are a pale creamy yellow colour and the forewing is marked by a pair of brown vertical lines, with only one similar line on the hindwing. The hindwing tails are emphasized by small brown spots at the base.

CATERPILLAR: Slender, brown body with pale side stripes. Feeds on hawthorn, ivy and privet
WINGSPAN: 5–6.5cm
HABITAT: Hedgerows, woodland, parks, gardens and commons
RANGE: Across Europe into temperate Asia
STATUS: Relatively common

EASTERN TENT CATERPILLAR MOTH
MALACOSOMA AMERICANUM

CATERPILLAR: Dark grey, hairy body with blue and red patches. Feeds on a variety of tree and shrub leaves
WINGSPAN: 4–5cm
HABITAT: Deciduous woodland, orchards, parks and gardens
RANGE: Across the eastern half of North America, from southern Canada into the United States
STATUS: Common and widespread

This moth is a member of the Lasiocampidae family, commonly referred to as lappet moths, which have no tongues, connected wings and generally hairy bodies. The Eastern Tent Caterpillar Moth shows all these characteristics: its stout body is covered in brown hair. Its wings are solid brown in colour, varying from a peachy light colour to much darker; however, all varieties have a pair of distinctive white stripes across the forewing and these are often infilled with white, creating a broad, pale band. The caterpillars live communally in white, silken tents, hence its common name.

GASTROPACHA QUERCIFOLIA LAPPET MOTH

Like most Lasiocampid moths, the Lappet Moth has a stocky body which is also furry. It is a rich red-brown colour throughout and the wings can appear to have a purplish sheen. Both the forewings and the hindwings are marked with delicate brown lines which are slightly scalloped. The wings themselves are broadly scalloped, the forewings larger than the rounded hindwings. When the moth is at rest, it holds its wings more upright than most other moths, providing it with effective camouflague when amongst dead leaves. Males and females are similar although female is larger.

CATERPILLAR: Lumpy grey body with brown hairs. Feeds on hawthorn and blackthorn

WINGSPAN: 4–7.5cm

HABITAT: Woodland, forest clearings and hedgerows, parks and gardens

RANGE: From Europe into Asia, China and Japan

STATUS: Generally common

OAK EGGAR

LASIOCAMPA QUERCUS

The male Oak Eggar can be easily identified by its contrasting brown colouring on both wings. Towards the base it is a rich chocolate brown which is then edged with a broad marginal band of pale yellow-brown. Although the depth of the brown colouring can vary across its range, the forewing always bears a single black-ringed white spot. This marking also appears on the significantly larger female, whose wing colouring is much paler. Males fly during the day, whereas the female is nocturnal. The male can also be identified by his feathered antennae which enable him to find the scent of the female.

CATERPILLAR: Dark brown with black rings and orange hairs. Feeds on oak, brambles, hawthorn and heather
WINGSPAN: 5–9cm
HABITAT: Woodland, moorland, hedgerows
RANGE: Across Europe into north Africa
STATUS: Generally common

GYPSY MOTH

LYMANTRIA DISPAR

The Gypsy Moth is a daytime flier. However, observers will only ever see a male in flight: the female, although winged, does not fly at all, a typical characteristic of the Lymantriidae family. Males and females are very different: the male is smaller with mottled brown, orange and yellow forewings and solid yellow-brown hindwings which are bordered with white and dark brown chequering; the female has creamy white wings with simple dark markings on the forewings, including a characteristic V shape near the leading edges. The borders of both wings are chequered white and black. Her body is very large and when carrying a huge egg sac it doubles in size.

CATERPILLAR: Grey body with red and blue tufted spots along the back. Feeds voraciously on on oaks and other trees and shrubs
WINGSPAN: 4–6cm
HABITAT: Mature deciduous woodland, a variety of wooded areas, meadows, orchards, parks and gardens
RANGE: Widespread; native to Europe and Asia, introduced to North America in the nineteenth century.
STATUS: Very common. Considered a serious pest in North America

BLACK WITCH ASCALAPHA ODORATA

CATERPILLAR: Dark brown body. Feeds on cassia
WINGSPAN: 11–15cm
HABITAT: A variety of habitats, including woodland, meadows, parks and gardens
RANGE: Across North America, occasionally Canada, down towards Central America
STATUS: Common and widespread

Although a seemingly dull brown moth, the Black Witch has a number of distinguishing features. Its long, pointed forewing has a kidney-shaped eyespot towards the centre of the leading edge and this is coloured a metallic blue, a sharp contrast to the deep-brown-mottled wing. On the squared hindwing there is a large eyespot which is sharply toothed towards the outer margin and this too is suffused with metallic-blue scales. The scalloped hindwing edges are bordered with darker brown bands. Females have a slightly pinkish band that runs across both wings. The Black Witch is a strong flier, like most Noctuid moths, and will migrate long distances.

THYSANIA AGRIPPINA GIANT AGRIPPA

This striking, broad-winged moth has the widest wingspan of any moth in the world – indeed of any butterfly. Its wings are a grey-white colour marked with delicate and intricate dark brown lines and chevrons. Both wings are gently scalloped and the margins are lined with deeper, brown scallops, the pattern of which is repeated up through to the base of the wings. Close to the leading edge of the forewing is a small, distinctive brown eyespot, which appears rather square. Its pale body is banded with dark brown.

CATERPILLAR: Feeds on leguminous plants
WINGSPAN: 23–30cm
HABITAT: Tropical and subtropical forest and woodland
RANGE: Across Central and South America to southern Brazil
STATUS: Generally common

PUSS MOTH CERURA VINULA

CATERPILLAR: Bright green body with dark purple saddle in centre of back. Feeds on willow, sallow and poplar

WINGSPAN: 6–8cm

HABITAT: Open woodland, parks and gardens, often close to water

RANGE: Across Europe into Asia

STATUS: Widespread and common

The Puss is a member of the Notodontidae or 'Prominent' family, whose moths have long forewings, which are often tufted with fine scales. The Puss Moth is perhaps less remarkable than its caterpillar. Its forewings are patterned with a zig-zag marbling of buff-brown and grey, whereas its grey-brown hindwings lack markings other than darker veins. Its long, broad body is furred with a striped abdomen and at the base of the forewings are white scales. Its striking caterpillar effectively deals with predators by whipping out long pink filaments from its forked tails and by squirting formic acid from its throat. When threatened it raises its head, showing a pink 'face' with false 'eyes'.

PTEROPHORUS PENTADACTYLA WHITE PLUME MOTH

This pure-white moth is a member of the Pterophoridae family, commonly known as plume moths since their wings have the appearance of fine feathers. The White Plume Moth has a typical forewing that is divided into two lobes or 'plumes', whilst its hindwing is divided into three. The lobes are covered with scales, just as those of other Lepidoptera are, and the addition of long fringe scales on each lobe adds to the feathery effect. The White Plume Moth holds its wings out when it rests, adopting a T shape; this is accentuated by its proportionally long, white hind legs, which trail alongside its abdomen.

CATERPILLAR: Olive-colour body with yellow stripe along back and short spines. Feeds on bindweed

WINGSPAN: 2.5–3.5cm

HABITAT: Open grassland, hedgerows, roadsides, gardens

RANGE: Across Europe into Asia

STATUS: Widespread and common

INDIAN MEAL MOTH

PLODIA INTERPUNCTELLA

The Indian Meal Moth is a member of the Pyralid family, known primarily as pest moths since their caterpillars will live amongst and consume stored grain products. The tiny nocturnal moth is attracted to light and can be seen flying inside houses. Its forewings are a copper colour with pale grey towards the base. The hindwings are mottled grey and the body is a brownish grey. Its larvae eat a variety of stored products from cereals and grain to dried fruits, pet foods and powdered milk. As it feeds its spins a silken thread which sticks food particles together in webs. It will also leave behind shed skin casts and its faeces, or frass. Caterpillars can often be seen hanging from ceilings on a single thread of silk.

CATERPILLAR: Pale body with black head
WINGSPAN: 1.5–2cm
HABITAT: Warehouses and most large food-storage facilities, kitchens and pantries
RANGE: Across North America, Europe and into Asia
STATUS: Very common

REGAL MOTH

CITHERONIA REGALIS

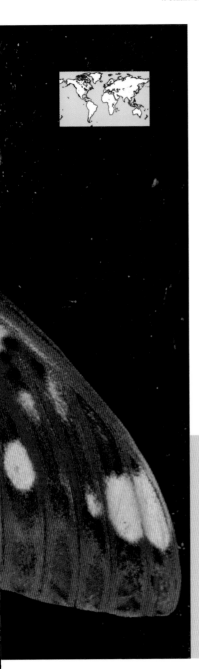

This attractive moth is known as both the Regal and the Royal Walnut Moth, and is a widespread representative of the Saturnid family in North America. Its forewings have a background colour of grey-brown which is marked with ruddy orange veins, between some of which are pale yellow spots. The paler hindwing is more orange with smaller areas of grey towards the outer edge and a suffusion of yellow at the inner edge and base. Its large furred body is orange with pale yellow bands on the abdomen and yellow markings on the head and thorax. Its inability to feed means it only lives for a few days. Its slightly alarming caterpillar is commonly known as the Hickory Horned Devil.

CATERPILLAR: Green body with large branching head horns. Feeds on hickory and other broad leaves
WINGSPAN: 9–16cm
HABITAT: Woodland, forests, parks and gardens
RANGE: Across eastern states of the USA
STATUS: Generally common

PROMETHEA MOTH CALLOSAMIA PROMETHEAN

CATERPILLAR: Green body with four red horns on the back of the head and a red tail horn. Feeds on a variety of trees, including sassafras, poplar and cherry
WINGSPAN: 7.5–10cm
HABITAT: Deciduous forests, open woodland, orchards
RANGE: Eastern USA and south-east Canada
STATUS: Generally common

This American Saturnid or emperor moth comes in two distinctive sex forms. The males are a purplish-black colour with a pale brown or tan border along both wings. The females are a red-brown colour with pale wavy bands across both wings, a pale border marked with reddish lines on the forewing and a broken band on the hindwing. The female's body is red-brown and stocky, whereas the male's is slender and black. Both sexes bear a distinctive black eyespot with blue and white highlights in the tip of the forewing. Males fly during the afternoon and females at night – they meet to mate at dusk.

AUTOMERIS IO IO MOTH

Although the sexes of the Io Moth are coloured differently, both bear startling eyespots on the hindwing which are effectively used to deter predators. When threatened, the Io Moth lifts its forewings to flash its 'eyes'. The smaller male is coloured yellow on both wings, the pointed forewing has fine wavy lines of pale brown while the hindwing has a pair of parallel bands around the marginal edge. The large black and blue eyespot is in the centre of the hindwing. The female has solid pale brown forewings and similar-coloured hindwings, but with a broad white marginal band and a single black line around the eyespot.

CATERPILLAR: Pale green with stinging yellow spines in clusters along the back and red and white side stripes. Feeds on a variety of plants
WINGSPAN: 5–8.5cm
HABITAT: Deciduous forests, open woodland, scrubland, fields and gardens
RANGE: From Canada into the USA towards Mexico
STATUS: Widespread and generally common

ATLAS MOTH

ATTACUS ATLAS

Although not as broad-winged as the Giant Agrippa Moth, the wings of the Atlas Moth have the biggest surface area, making this the world's largest moth. It is as distinctive as it is huge: the rich-brown wings are marked with fine white bands and translucent white triangular patches; the outer margins of both wings are paler brown with dark streaks and spots along the margin. The forewing tip is deeply curved and its patterning strongly resembles a snake's head with a small eyespot, a red slash for the mouth and pale shading. This deliberate feature deters predators very effectively. The caterpillar is almost as enormous as its moth, often reaching up to 12cm in length.

CATERPILLAR: Green body with long spines covered with white sticky powder. Feeds on a variety of tree foliage, including willow and poplar
WINGSPAN: 16–30cm
HABITAT: Tropical and subtropical woodland
RANGE: From India and Sri Lanka, across Indonesia to China
STATUS: Locally common, though numbers are declining

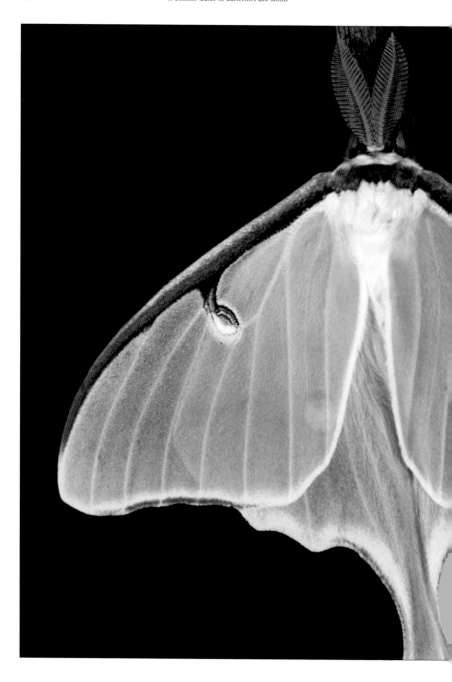

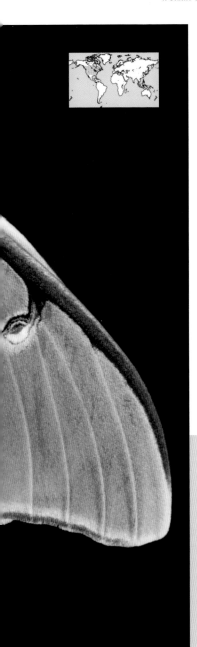

AMERICAN MOON MOTH

ACTIAS LUNA

This American member of the Actias sub-family is a beautiful and exotic moth, with its pale green wings and long, delicate tail streamers. It has relatively broad and stocky wings which are edged with red along both fore- and hindwings. The background colour of the wings can vary between different regions, from a more yellow to a more blue green. The leading edge of the forewing is more broadly edged with dark, purplish grey. Both wings bear distinctive eyespots which earn it both its common and its scientific name. The sexes are similar, but the male's antennae are feathered. Mating pairs will often stay in position for up to twenty hours.

CATERPILLAR: Green body with raised pink spots. Feeds on tree foliage including alder, willow and birch
WINGSPAN: 7.5–11cm
HABITAT: Deciduous woodland
RANGE: Across North America, though fewer in Canada
STATUS: Generally common

INDIAN MOON MOTH Actias selene

Caterpillar: Pale green body with red raised spots bearing black spines; two yellow spots on the head. Feeds on a variety of trees and shrubs, including rhododendron

Wingspan: 8–12cm

Habitat: Tropical and subtropical woodland

Range: Across Asia into China

Status: Numerous in captivity, generally common in the wild

The Indian Moon Moth is a particular favourite of collectors and enthusiasts, and this has affected its numbers in the wild. Like all other Saturnid or emperor moths, this moth has no mouthparts and therefore lives for less than a week. It is however a striking moth and like the American Moon Moth has beautiful long tail streamers and pale yellow-green wings with distinctive eyespots. Its forewing is relatively narrow and slightly more pointed, edged with yellow on the outer margins and along the leading edge with reddish purple. The hindwing outer edge is more broadly yellow and this is continued down into the tail, which also bears a pinkish blush. The eyespots have a characteristic moon-like appearance.

SATURNIA PYRI GREAT PEACOCK MOTH

This big Saturnid moth is Europe's largest moth and is generally observed only in southern areas. It is mainly brown in colouring, with a rich brown background colour on both wings. The forewing is dusted with white scales at the leading edge and the centre; a dark band separates this from the solid brown base of the wing. A pale wavy band across the centre of the forewing is repeated on the hindwing below the eyespot. The outer margins of both wings are bordered with white and buff. The hindwing is paler at the base and darker brown towards the outer edge. A black eyespot ringed with brown and black and highlighted white sits at the centre of each wing.

CATERPILLAR: Pale green body with white side stripe, and raised hairy green spots. Feeds on fruit-tree foliage

WINGSPAN: 10–15cm

HABITAT: Open woodland, orchards, gardens

RANGE: Southern Europe, into north Africa and Asia

STATUS: Common, considered a pest in orchards

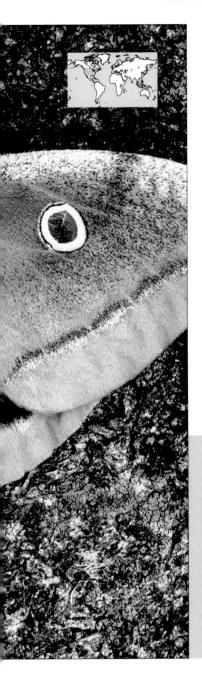

POLYPHEMUS MOTH

ANTHERAEA POLYPHEMUS

In Greek mythology, Polyphemus was the giant with a single, all-seeing eye. The Polyphemus Moth is also particularly large with a very distinctive eyespot on the hindwing. The wing colour varies from a pale yellow-brown to darker red-brown; the pattern is however regular. On both wings towards the base is a fine red line margined with white and towards the outer margins another fine brown line. The forewing bears a small white eyespot ringed with black and two dark patches at the tip. The hindwing has a large grey eyespot containing a yellow oval and ringed with black. The Polyphemus Moth is the most common member of the Saturnid family found in North America.

CATERPILLAR: Pale green body with raised red spots from which grow hairs. Feeds on tree foliage, particularly apple and hawthorn
WINGSPAN: 10–13cm
HABITAT: A variety, including deciduous forests, desert canyons, scrubland and suburban gardens
RANGE: Widespread across North America
STATUS: Generally common

EMPEROR MOTH
SATURNIA PAVONIA

CATERPILLAR: Pale green body with raised spots and yellow hairs. Feeds on heather, bramble and hawthorn
WINGSPAN: 5.5–9cm
HABITAT: Open woodland and clearings, meadows, heathland, moorland and scrub
RANGE: Across Europe into Scandinavia
STATUS: Widespread and common

This daytime-flying, temperate moth can appear in different colour forms in different areas; however all varieties share several key features. The background colour of the Emperor Moth is either brown, light or dark, or a grey-brown, slightly mottled to enable camouflage. The outer margins of the forewing bear a broad white band, and the edge of the hindwing also has a pale border. A prominent eyespot is borne on each wing; the forewing eyespot sits on a contrasting patch of white whilst the hindwing eyespot sits on either a white or yellow patch depending on the variety. Like all Saturnid moths, the male has feathery antennae with which he can detect the scent of the female, often from a distance of two kilometres.

CECROPIA/ROBIN MOTH
HYALOPHORA CECROPIA

Most Saturnid moths are able to produce silk, though not of the quality of the Bombycid moths, and in the USA the family is often referred to as Giant Silkmoths. The Cecropia is one of the biggest found in North America. It is an attractive brown and red moth; the background colour of both wings is brown, with pale borders and a series of dark spots on the margin of the forewing which terminate at the tip with an eyespot. It has a crescent marking the centre of each wing, and this is invariably white marked with red. A white and red band runs across both wings and the body is furred red, with a small white collar behind the head.

CATERPILLAR: Green with yellow back horns and blue markings. Feeds on tree and shrub foliage
WINGSPAN: 11–15cm
HABITAT: Woodland, orchards, parks and gardens
RANGE: Widespread from Canada through USA
STATUS: Locally common, although declining as a result of pesticide use

HORNET MOTH

SESIA APIFORMIS

The Sesiidae family are best known for their mimicry of wasps, and the Hornet Moth is a particularly convincing example. Its large furred abdomen is striped with bands of yellow and black, and it has a yellow head and a black thorax edged with yellow sides. Its thickened antennae closely resemble those of a true hornet, as do its long, thick, brown hind legs. The Hornet Moth has transparent wings, typical for its family; the only wing scales are found on the brown edges. Although this is a daytime moth, it is rarely observed and its tree-boring caterpillar is widely considered a pest.

CATERPILLAR: Creamy white body. Feeds on the trunks and roots of poplar trees, taking up to two years to pupate
WINGSPAN: 3–4.5cm
HABITAT: Mature woodland, wooded marshland and river valleys
RANGE: Across Europe into Asia, North America
STATUS: More common in warmer areas

DEATH'S HEAD HAWK MOTH
ACHERONTIA ATROPOS

CATERPILLAR: Yellow body with blue-green bands and black side spots. Yellow tail spine. Feeds on potato leaves and deadly nightshade
WINGSPAN: 10–13cm
HABITAT: Agricultural land, particularly potato fields; open grassland
RANGE: Across southern Europe into north Africa
STATUS: Generally common

This well known – indeed, infamous – moth earns its name from the unusual markings on its thorax, which resemble an image of a skull. It is the largest European example of a hawk or Sphingidae (sphinx) moth, a family of particulary large, powerful and fast fliers. Its forewings are dark brown mottled with light patches, and when at rest these cover the abdomen and the brighter, yellow hindwings. These are edged with a pair of brown bands, one broad and one fine, and this colouring is repeated on the abdomen, which is banded brown and yellow with a central back band in brown. Like its relative it has a long strong tongue, with which it can pierce beehives in search of honey. When threatened it will chirp.

HUMMINGBIRD CLEARWING

HEMARIS THYSBE

An attractive daytime moth, this American hummingbird moth closely resembles its European relative in all but its wings and its tail shape. Its body is a furred rusty brown colour, with the lower part of the abdomen ringed with black and deep brown, terminating in a pointed, tufted tail. Its wings are clear, with dark, scaled tips and borders and black veining. The base of the wings is olive-green. The European *Macroglossum stellatarum* has solid-brown forewings, orange hindwings and a fanned tail. Both species so closely resemble hummingbirds when hovering in front of flowers that they are regularly mistaken for tiny birds.

CATERPILLAR: Green body with green and yellow tail horn. Feeds on hawthorn, viburnum and honeysuckle

WINGSPAN: 4–6cm

HABITAT: Open fields, meadows, hedgerows, roadsides

RANGE: Widespread from Alaska and Canada, through eastern USA to Colorado

STATUS: Very common

CAROLINA SPHINX

MANDUCA SEXTA

The wings of the Carolina Sphinx are mainly grey, mottled with black and white. This slightly dull appearance provides the moth with excellent camouflage against tree bark and rock. The hindwings have a more streaked pattern; however it is the abdomen that gives the moth is distinctive appearance, bearing six pairs of square yellow patches. The caterpillar of this moth is well known as a serious pest: it focuses particularly on plants such as tobacco, potato and tomato and can attack crops in large numbers. It is for this reason that its pupa is commonly known as the tobacco hornworm.

CATERPILLAR: Green body with white side stripes and a red tail horn
WINGSPAN: 10–12cm
HABITAT: Open farmland, scrubland and gardens
RANGE: Across the Americas, from northern states of the USA into South America
STATUS: Widespread and common

WEBBING/ COMMON CLOTHES MOTH

TINEOLA BISSELLIELLA

This tiny moth is capable of a great deal of destruction when left unchecked. Although the moth itself is not a pest, its larvae feed on all keratin-based materials such as wool, hair and silk, as well as cotton, stored grain and cereals. It therefore eats not only clothes, but carpets and upholstery. As the larva feeds it weaves silken tubes and webs, inside which it lives, hence its other common name. The moth itself has pale, creamy wings and a similarly coloured body. Its head is covered with red hair and it has proportionally long antennae. These moths are now rarely seen in houses, partly due to the drying effects of central heating and the extensive use of man-made fibres.

CATERPILLAR: Pale, whitish body with brown head
WINGSPAN: 1–2cm
HABITAT: In birds' nests and small animal dens. In cupboards, pipe lagging or under carpets
RANGE: Across the northern hemisphere
STATUS: Widespread and common, though numbers in decline

MADAGASCAN SUNSET MOTH

CHRYSIRIDIA RIPHEARIA

This spectacular moth is a member of the Uraniid family; not only is it brightly coloured with iridescent scaling and tail streamers, it is also a daytime flier and so is regularly mistaken for a butterfly. Found only on the island of its name, the Madagascan Sunset Moth has black forewings marked with luminous blue-green streaks and patches. The hindwings bear the 'sunset', a red and orange patch which diffuses into a pale blue streak across the wing. The colours on the hindwing are marked with black patches and spots and the white streamers are lined with black. This moth has been highly sought after by collectors for hundreds of years, and during the nineteenth century its wings were often used to decorate jewellery.

CATERPILLAR: Yellow and black body with black hairs. Feeds on poisonous euphorbia plants
WINGSPAN: 8–10cm
HABITAT: Tropical forests
RANGE: Confined to Madagascar
STATUS: Locally common

BUTTERFLIES

Like all other living organisms, Lepidoptera are divided into families, groupings of butterflies and moths which share certain key characteristics. There are currently 127 families of moths and butterflies, and of the butterflies there are five major families which are detailed here.

Papilionidae: Swallowtails

This family contains some of the largest and most boldly marked species of butterfly, and although most are native to tropical habitats some can be found in temperate climates. Many of the Papilionidae have long 'tails' on their hindwings – hence the popular name 'swallowtails' – which are generally used to distract predators from attacking the butterfly's body. With their large wings, swallowtails are strong fliers and can often be seen several metres above the ground. Their striking and beautiful appearance makes them particularly attractive to collectors so many species under threat of extinction are subject to international protection orders.

Pieridae: Whites and Sulphurs

The Pierid family consists mainly of whites, marbles and sulphurs, and its members can be found around the world. They are generally medium-sized butterflies with simple markings. Males and females are often dissimilar or dimorphic, and while both sexes can be seen visiting flowers for nectar, groups observed visiting water tend to be exclusively male. Peirids tend to fly in open sunny areas and are on the wing during the summer and early autumn. Their caterpillars are voracious eaters and can devour whole host plants, particularly when feeding together. As a result many species are considered pests and one of the best known members of the family is the Large White or Cabbage White, the nemesis of gardeners everywhere.

Lycaenidae: Gossamer Wings

This is a large family consisting of mainly small, brilliantly coloured butterflies, often referred to as the Gossamer Wings. Many Lycaenidae have a metallic sheen on their upper wings, particularly those belong to the Blues. The group known as Hairstreaks often have tails on their hindwings, while Coppers are usually bright red or orange with striking markings.

The caterpillars of most Lycaenidae also tend to be small and may resemble tiny snails. Many caterpillars of the Blue group have an unusual association with a species of ant: when small they allow themselves to be taken into the ants' nest, where they secrete a sweet fluid appealing to the ant. In return the caterpillars help themselves to ant larva, which provides them with a rich source of protein. In order to keep the ants at bay, the caterpillar emits a clicking noise; after hatching from its chrysalis, the butterfly leaves the nest while the ants are inactive.

Below: Sulphur butterflies are members of the Pieridae family.

The selection of butterflies here also includes members of the Riodinidae family, or Metalmarks. Most species of this family are found in the South American tropics and, as their common name suggests, many are decorated with gold, silver and copper metallic scales.

Nymphalidae: Brushfoots

This is the largest and most diverse butterfly family, with over 6,000 known species worldwide. Commonly referred to as Brushfoots, these butterflies can appear to have only four legs; the final pair of legs are much smaller, often hairy, and are adapted for cleaning the butterfly's antennae and body instead of walking. Many species share distinctive flight behaviour, flapping and gliding instead of fluttering, while others are noted for feeding on the juices of rotten plants, fruit and even animals. Nymphalidae cover a range of sizes and appearance and contain sub-families such as the fritillaries, monarchs, emperors, tortoiseshells and admirals.

Hesperiidae: Skippers

These small butterflies are generally recognized by their flight behaviour, skipping rapidly from flower to flower. European skippers are usually small with dull colours, whereas their tropical relatives can appear bolder and brightly coloured. They have large, stout bodies and broad heads, and the antenna often lack the clubbed ends of most other butterfly species. The caterpillars of skippers live in spun tubes attached to host plants, which protect them from predators. Skippers are believed to be the most primitive butterfly family, with over 3,000 members.

Satyridae: Browns and Satyrs

As the common name of this family suggests, all Satyridae have some kind of brown colouring. They are generally inconspicuous, flying low in search of food such as rotting fruit and honeydew; however they can be observed basking in bright sunlight. All Satyridae, however patterned above, bear at least one eyespot on their underside; this is their main form of defence, since they are not generally poisonous.

Opposite: The Athis Longwing (Heliconius athis) is a member of the Nymphalidae family.

MOTHS

Of the 127 currently recognized families of Lepidoptera, most are moths. As with butterflies, they vary enormously, ranging from small experts in camouflage to large and dramatic daytime fliers such as the Uraniids, and only a small selection can be described here.

Arctiid moths

This group contains over 10,000 species worldwide,and comprises two distinct groups of butterflies known as Tiger moths and Ermines. Their bright colours and eye-catching patterning has earned the first group the popular name of Tiger moths. The colouring of these species is a sign of their poisonous status, as with the butterflies, these displays act as a warning to potential predators. Ermines, as their name suggests, are pale with black spots.

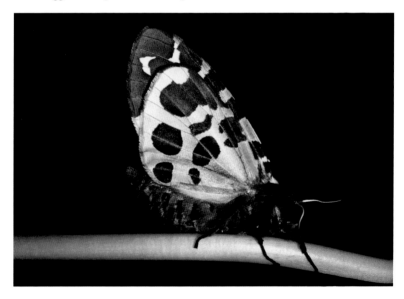

Bombycid and Saturnid moths

These are more commonly known as silkmoths, a family which includes the species which has been important to human societies for thousands of years. Emerging Bombycid moths lack mouth parts and are unable to feed, relying on the energy stored during the caterpillar stage. Another family of silkmoths is the Saturnid, or emperor moths, large and attractive species, many of which spin a coarse silk for their cocoons which can be harvested for human use.

Brahmaeid and Noctuidae moths

Brahmaeid moths are large macro moths, usually displaying large eyespots which earn some member species the title of owl moths. Also known as owl moths are the Noctuid family, although this is due to their nocturnal behaviour. Unlike the Brahmaeid moths, Noctuids can range between small micro moths, to larger macro

*Opposite: Garden Tiger Moth (*Arctia caja*) settled on stem.*
*Above: Golden Emperor Moth (*Loepa katinka*) is a member of the Saturnid family and is found from North India to China.*

Above: Some species belonging to the Shingidae family can easily be mistaken for other insects such as wasps.
*Opposite: Caterpillar of the Gypsy Moth (*Lymantria dispar*)which is a threat to forest trees.*

moths, some can be drab and unremarkable, others as striking as butterflies. The Noctuidae is one of the largest families containing over 25,000 species and it also includes a number of highly destructive varieties of caterpillar. Similar to Noctuid moths, but often slightly hairier, the Lymantrid moths. Within this group, only the male is capable of flight, the female is generally large bodied and immobile, with wings which cannot function.

Lasiocampid and Notodontid moths

These are stocky and often furry moths which unlike all others lack the wing-coupling device which distinguishes moths from butterflies. Their caterpillars are also hairy and they form egg shaped cocoons, hence the common name eggar moths. Another family distinguished by hairy features is the Notodontid, whose moths bear tufts of scales on the forewing which stand upright when the moth is at rest. As a result these moths are usually referred to as prominents.

Sphingidae moths

Better known as Hawk moths, the family Sphingidae consists of around 1,000 members. These are distinguished by their fast powerful flight and their particularly long tongues or proboscis. A number of Hawk moths resemble other species of insect and even birds, such as the Hummingbird Clearwing. Another family that contains effective mimics is the Sesiidae, which particularly favour wasps and hornets as models.

Geometrid moths

The second largest family of moths is the Geometrid, with over 15,000 species found worldwide. These moths are often slender bodied and weak fliers, many rely on camouflage for survival, although there are, of course, some exceptions. Their caterpillars are popularly known as inchworms or loopers for their method of drawing up the centre of their body in order to move forwards, having legs only at the head and tail ends.

Caterpillars

Moths themselves are rarely pests, it is their caterpillars which can do damage and Pyralidae and the Tineidae families are represented here by their most infamous member species. Pyralid larva feed on stored grains and other foodstuff, whilst the Tineidae caterpillars in the wild will feed on animal detritus, funghi and lichen, and once inside human homes will consume natural fibres such as cotton and wool.

GLOSSARY

ABDOMEN The segmented tail area of a butterfly or moth. The abdomen contains the heart, Malpighian tubules, reproductive organs, and most of the digestive system. It is protected by an exoskeleton. The abdomen of butterflies and moths has eleven segments, with the terminal 2 or 3 segments fused together.

ANTENNAE Sensory appendages (singular antenna) on the head of some adult insects, which are used for the sense of smell and balance. Butterflies have two segmented antennae with a small club at the end of each. Moths have antennae without the club. Larvae (caterpillars) have tiny sensory antennae.

ARMY The term for a group of caterpillars.

BASKING Butterflies bask in the sun when their body temperature becomes too low, because when they are too cold they cannot fly. They sun themselves with outstretched wings in order to absorb as much heat as possible.

BIODIVERSITY The abundance of different plant and animal species found in an environment.

BLUES A group of butterflies that belong to the family Lycaenidae.

Most blues have some type of relationship with ants.

BROOD A single generation of butterflies that live during the same time period.

CATERPILLAR The larval stage of butterflies and moths. Caterpillars eat almost constantly and moult many times as they grow.

CHRYSALIS The pupa of a butterfly, derived from the Greek word for gold.

COCOON A protective covering, made of silk, which protects a moth pupa (and some other insects). The cocoon is spun from the abdomen of the larva (caterpillar) before it pupates.

EYE SPOT A circular, eye-like marking found on the wings of some butterflies or the body of some caterpillars, which make the insect look like the face of a much larger animal and may scare away some predators.

FAMILY In classification, a family is a group of related or similar organisms. A family contains one or more genera (plural of genus). A group of similar families forms an order.

FILAMENTS Some caterpillars have

filaments (also known as tentacles) on their bodies. These fleshy appendages provide sensory information for the caterpillar and are often mistaken for antennae. Monarch caterpillars have two pairs of filaments.

FOREWINGS The two upper wings of a butterfly or moth.

GENUS In classification, a genus is a group of related or similar organisms. A genus contains one or more species. A group of similar genera (the plural of genus) forms a family. In the scientific name of an organism, the first name is its genus.

HERBIVORE Animals that eat plants – most butterflies are herbivores.

HINDWINGS The two lower wings of a butterfly or moth.

HONEYDEW A sweet chemical solution that some caterpillars (and other insects, like aphids) secrete in order to attract and feed other insects (like ants).

IMAGO The adult stage of an insect (like a butterfly or moth) during which the insect reproduces.

INSECTIVORE An organism that eats mostly insects – many birds are insectivores.

INVERTEBRATE Animals that do not have a backbone, such as butterflies and moths.

LARVA The caterpillar stage in the life cycle of a butterfly or moth.

LEGS Butterflies and moth, like other insects, have six legs in their adult stage. These three pairs of legs are attached to the thorax, one pair in each segment of the thorax.

LEPIDOPTERA Lepidoptera (scale wing) is an order of insects characterized by having four large, scaly wings and a spiral proboscis. Butterflies and moths belong to the order Lepidoptera. There are about 150,000 named species of butterflies and moth (over 87 per cent are moths).

LEPIDOPTERIST A scientist who studies butterflies and moths.

LIFE CYCLE Butterflies and moths go through four different life stages: the egg, larva (caterpillar), pupa, and adult.

MANDIBLES The jaws of the caterpillar and many other insects. The mandibles bite off plant material and tear it into small, easily digestible pieces. Adult butterflies do not have mandibles.

METAMORPHOSIS Metamorphosis is the transformation of an animal during its life cycle. Butterflies and moths undergo complete metamorphosis, which is the complete reorganization of the tissues of an animal during its life cycle, usually involving the addition of legs and wings. The larval stage of butterflies and moths (the caterpillar) metamorphoses into a winged, flying adult (the adult butterfly or moth).

MIGRATION The movement of a large group of an animal species across many miles to avoid adverse conditions. Many butterflies migrate in order to avoid cold weather, although it is not well understood. Most migrate relatively short distances but a few (like the Monarch and the Painted Lady) migrate thousands of miles.

MIMICRY When two unrelated species have similar markings.

Batesian mimicry is when a non-poisonous species has markings similar to a poisonous species and gains protection from this similarity. Müllerian mimicry is when two poisonous species have similar markings; fewer insects need to be sacrificed in order to teach the predators not to eat these unpalatable animals. An example is the poisonous Queen butterfly, which mimics the poisonous Monarch.

MORPH A variety of a species that is easily distinguished For example, there may be two colour morphs of a species of butterfly.

MOTH Winged insects that belong to the Order Lepidoptera. Moths have feathered antennae (not clubbed antennae like butterflies), a frenulum or jugum, and are generally dull coloured. There are over 100,000 moth species alive today.

NECTAR The sweet liquid produced by many flowers. Adult butterflies sip nectar through their proboscis.

NOCTURNAL Most active at night – many moths are nocturnal.

ORDER In classification, an order is a group of related or similar organisms. An order contains one or more families. A group of similar orders forms a class. Butterflies and moths belong to the Order Lepidoptera.

OVERWINTERING Also called hibernation, this is a condition in which an animal is dormant for period of time. Some butterflies and moths overwinter during cold weather.

OVIPAROUS An animal that hatches from an egg. Butterflies and moths are oviparous and usually lay their eggs on leaves of the plant that the larva (caterpillar) will eat.

OVIPOSITOR An organ at the end of the female's abdomen through which she deposits her eggs.

PHEROMONE Chemicals secreted by some animals that cause specific reactions in other animals. Some animals, like moths, use pheromones to attract mates.

PREPUPA The last larval stage of an insect after it stops eating. During this period, it is resting, looks shrivelled up and may even appear to be dead.

PROBOSCIS A tube-like, flexible 'tongue' that butterflies and moths use to sip their liquid food (usually flower nectar or the liquid from rotting fruits). The proboscis uncoils to sip food, and coils up again into a spiral when not in use. It consists of two halves joined together. The hawk moth has the longest proboscis.

PUPA The stage in a butterfly's (or moth's) life when it is encased in a chrysalis and undergoing metamorphosis. It does not eat during this stage and is outwardly inactive, but a lot is going on inside; the caterpillar is changing into a butterfly. The pupa stage lasts from a few days to many months (some butterflies overwinter in the pupa stage, and the adult emerges in the spring).

PUPATE To turn into and exist as a pupa.

RABBLE A group of butterflies, also known as a swarm.

SEGMENTS The natural sections that an insect's body is divided into. The abdomens of butterflies and moths have eleven segments – the terminal 2 or 3 segments are fused together.

SEXUAL DIMORPHISM The physical differences between the males and females of a species. Frequently, male and female butterflies are distinguished by vein width and other characteristics.

SWARM A group of butterflies also called a rabble.

THORA The chest area of a butterfly or moth. The thorax is divided into three segments; on each segment is a pair of legs. The four wings of the butterfly (or moth) are also attached to the thorax and it contains the muscles that make the legs and wings move.

VEINS The rib-like tubes in the wings of butterflies and moths that support the wings and bring nourishment to them.

VENATION The vein pattern in the wings of butterflies and moths.

WINGS Butterflies and moths have four wings made of two layers which are nourished and supported by tubular veins.

WINGSPAN The distance measured across the wings.

INDEX

PICTURE CREDITS

The publisher would like to thank the following photographers and picture agencies for their kind permission to reproduce their images in this book:

ARDEA

21, 42, 54, 247 John Cancalosi (18/19) Auscape/Densey Clyne (34) Pascal Goetgheluck (36, 59, 104, 105, 121, 218/219, 222, 224/225) JB &S Bottomley (37, 145, 154) Bob Gibbons (1, 43, 50, 75, 80, , 85, 90/91, 92, 120, 130, 136, 137, 160, 182/3, 184, 185, 184, 186/187) Johan de Meester (46, 88, 110) Jack Bailey (47, 72/73, 114, 132/133, 161, 230) John Mason (48/49, 70, 72/73, 77, 78, 81, 93, 114, 124, 128, 132/133, 142/143, 144, 152, 161, 165, 166/167, 172, 174/175, 178, 179, 182/3, 185, 193, 206, 210, 216, 223, 228/229, 230) Dr Steve Hopkin (51, 52/53, 82, 141, 234/5) Duncan Usher (39, 56/57/98/126/127, 131, 226) Eric Dragesco (60/61) John Daniels (62/63) Donald Burgess (100/101) Alan Weaving (101/103, 125) Chris Martin Bahr (106/107) Brian Kenney (112/113) Gary W Carter (115, 192) M. Watson (116/117) Ian Beames (164, 173, 180/181, 190/191) Paul Van Gaalen (168) Martin B Withers (188, 189, 203, 204/205) Wardene Weeser (194/195) Joanna Van Gruisen (196/197) Bill Coster (211) Jack Swedberg (220/221)

OXFORD SCIENTIFIC FILMS:

214/215, 232/233 Stan Schroeder (99) Frithjof Skibbe (134/135) Stan Osolinski (169) Animals Animals (170/171) Larry Crowhurst 162/163) John Mitchell (108/109) David Fox (84, 199) Michael Fogden (64/65) Brian Kenney (30/31, 66/67, 71) Geoff Kidd (44/45) James Robinson (55) John Woolmer (58) Larry F Jernigan (74, 122/123) David Boag (3, 86/87) Bjorn Forsberg (89) Satoshi Kuribayashi (119) Ifa-Bilderteam Gmbh (68/69) Arthur Butler (200/201) Marty Cordano (208) OSF (209) Scott Camazine (212/213) Prof Jack Dermid (214/215) Tim Shepherd (232/233) Kjell Sandved (236/237)

CORBIS

Robert Pickett (198, 244, 245) Tony Wharton (94/95, 153) Joe McDonald (231), Lowell Georgia (202) Hans Reinhard (247)

CREATAS

2, 4, 5, 6, 7, 8, 9, 11, 12, 13, 14, 15, 16, 20, 22, 23, 24, 25, 26, 28, 29, 32, 33, 38, 40/41, 83, 96/97, 111, 118, 138/139, 140, 146/147, 148/149, 150/151, 156/157, 158/159, 176/177, 217, 227, 238/239, 241, 242, 246, 249, 250, 252

Front cover image: Ian Beames/Ardea   Back cover and back flap: Creatas

Thank you to Sophie Napier, Angela BlackwoodMurray, Elaine Morris and Matha Spearpoint at Ardea and Lorel Ward at Oxford Scientific Films for their help in producing this book. Thank you also to Simon Tayor.